THEODORE DREISER

In the same series:

Modern Literature Monographs

THEODORE DREISER

James Lundquist

Frederick Ungar Publishing Co.
New York

Second Printing, 1978
Copyright © 1974 by Frederick Ungar Publishing Co., Inc.
Printed in the United States of America
Library of Congress Catalog Card Number: 73-84600
Designed by Anita Duncan
ISBN: 0-8044-2563-9

Contents

Chronology

1871: Theodore Dreiser is born 27 August in Terre Haute, Indiana.

1879: Family breaks up; Dreiser accompanies his mother to Vincennes, Sullivan, and Evansville, Indiana.

1883: Dreiser and remaining family in Chicago, then to Warsaw, Indiana.

1887: He goes to Chicago to seek his fortune. Works at various menial jobs.

1889-1890: Dreiser attends Indiana University.

1890: His mother dies, 14 November.

1892: Dreiser gets job as reporter on Chicago *Globe*. In November is taken on as reporter by St. Louis *Globe-Democrat*.

1894: Dreiser journeys east, works for newspapers in Toledo, Cleveland, Pittsburgh.

1895: Moves to New York; becomes editor of *Ev'ry Month*.

1898: Marriage to Sallie White, a Missouri school-teacher.

1899: Starts writing *Sister Carrie* at friend Arthur Henry's home in Maumee, Ohio.

1900: Doubleday, Page and Company publish *Sister Carrie* but do not publicize it because of Mrs. Doubleday's objections to the moral attitudes in the novel.

1901-1903: Moves toward nervous breakdown; separates from wife. His brother Paul Dresser helps restore Dreiser by sending him to Muldoon's health camp in Westchester, New York.

1904:   Dreiser returns to literary work as fiction editor for Street and Smith publications.

1905:   Takes over editorship of *Smith's Magazine*.

1906:   Becomes editor of *Broadway Magazine*; death of Paul Dresser.

1907:   B. W. Dodge and Company republishes *Sister Carrie*, 18 May. Dreiser becomes editor of Butterick's *Delineator*, *New Idea Women's Magazine*, and *Designer*.

1909:   *Jennie Gerhardt* started seriously. Separates again from wife.

1910:   Loses job with Butterick because of involvement with daughter of a woman employee.

1911:   Harper and Brothers publish *Jennie Gerhardt*. Dreiser travels to Europe. First volume of A *Trilogy of Desire*.

1912:   Harper and Brothers publish *The Financier*, republish *Sister Carrie*.

1913:   The Century Company publishes A *Traveler at Forty*.

1914:   The second volume of A *Trilogy of Desire*, *The Titan*, published 15 May by John Lane Company after Harper's backs off.

1915:   Tours Indiana by automobile. *The "Genius"* published by John Lane.

1916:   *The "Genius"* attacked for obscenity. John Lane withdraws novel. Publishes A *Hoosier Holiday*.

1918:   Dreiser gets new publisher, Boni & Liveright. *Free and Other Stories*, *The Hand of the Potter*, and *Twelve Men* appear.

1919:   Begins affair with Helen Richardson, his cousin, with whom he goes to Hollywood. *An American Tragedy* begun.

1920:   Publishes philosophical essays, *Hey, Rub-A-Dub-Dub!*

1922:   Publishes *A Book About Myself*.

1925:   *An American Tragedy* comes out and Dreiser enjoys financial success.

1927:   Travels through Russia.

1928:   Returns from Russia in January. Boni & Liveright publishes *Dreiser Looks at Russia*.

1929:   Publishes *A Gallery of Women*.

1931:   Liveright brings out *Tragic America* and *Dawn*. Increasing political involvement.

1932-1934: Dreiser is a contributing editor of the *American Spectator*, edited by George Nathan and Ernest Boyd.

1939:   Writes introduction to *The Living Thoughts of Thoreau*, published by Longmans, Green.

1941:   *America Is Worth Saving* appears.

1942:   Wife dies, 1 October.

1944:   Dreiser given Award of Merit by American Academy of Arts and Letters. Marries Helen Richardson 13 June.

1945:   Joins Communist Party. Dies in Hollywood, 28 December.

1946:   Doubleday publishes *The Bulwark*.

1947:   Doubleday publishes *The Stoic*, the last volume of *A Trilogy of Desire*.

1

Dreiser

Himself

Life is so treacherous, so sad!
—"Laughing Gas"

Theodore Dreiser's achievement as a writer is generally understood in terms of the despair, futility, and moral negativism concentrated in most of what he wrote. Whether in a minor and unproducible short play such as "Laughing Gas" or in *An American Tragedy*, one of our grimmest and most significant novels, his characters painfully discover that love is an illusion, that it is easy to wind up alone and abandoned, and that body chemistry has a greater influence on events than do abstractions such as conscience, mind, or spirit.

Dreiser's family background, his own disposition, and the era in which he grew up sufficiently validated the dark outlook and brooding style inevitably associated with him. For him, this view of life was more than a matter of artistic method or mawkish philosophizing. To a large extent his behavior reflected the belief that life is a jungle, that man is an animal manipulated by desire and instinct, and motivated solely by cupidity, pugnacity, vanity, and pleasure seeking. Yet strangely enough, despite the gloom found in his life and work, his richness of language and his powerful enthusiasm for and curiosity about human existence leave the student of Dreiser with anything but a surfeit of despair. Though Dreiser toughmindedly emphasizes the treachery of life, he also recognizes its sadness; and it is the compassion, not the toughness, that dominates in his writing.

This is not to say that Dreiser is divided in his artistry and wavers between depiction of life as a matter of brute force and sentimental evocation of his protagonists' unhappy fates. There is no need to qualify our conception of Dreiser as a relentless iconoclast determined to strip away popular illusions and make reticent critics and readers alike see life for the horrible thing it often is. What needs to be emphasized, how-

ever, is that in Dreiser's best work, as we shall see, the
treachery and sadness are seen as a simultaneous condition—indeed the only condition—of our existence.

Dreiser was born in Terre Haute, Indiana, on 27
August, 1871, a year after his parents' financial fortunes
had taken a fatal downward turn toward disaster. John
Dreiser, who was born in Germany and had entered
the United States some twenty-five years before Theodore's birth, operated a woolen mill in Sullivan, Indiana. Until 1869 his story had been a happy one; he
had acquired his own business in the classic American
way. Starting out as a weaver, he had become a production manager before finally going it on his own.
(The wife and eleven children acquired along the way
were a sure mark of success in the nineteenth century.)
But then the Dreiser mill was destroyed by fire at the
worst possible time—when it was full of consigned
fleeces. John Dreiser began to rebuild, but during con-
struction a beam fell, striking him on the head and
causing deafness in one ear. When shortly afterward,
his wife Sarah was cheated out of the family property,
John Dreiser was finished. He was never able to re-
establish himself, much less support his numerous
children. Dreiser consequently was raised in an atmosphere of constant poverty, looked after by a super-
stitious, ignorant (although loving) mother, and
terrorized by a defeated, often absent father, who grew,
as defeat followed defeat, more and more obsessed
with his Roman Catholic religion.

Although there was little love between Dreiser
and his father, the sudden reversal of John Dreiser's
hopes through no fault of his own, other than perhaps
ambition, made it impossible for Theodore to accept
the American dream of success. Even when Dreiser
had made a great deal of money from his writing, he

could not endorse the capitalist system and believed that, no matter how well things were going, he could be impoverished at any time. As long as he lived, Dreiser said several times, the approach of winter filled him with a sense of impending hunger and sickness.

Mrs. Dreiser did her best to keep the family going; but no matter how hard she worked taking in laundry and hiring out as a scrublady, there was a corrupting factor: sudden poverty, combined with the recollection of earlier affluence, awakened in the Dreiser children a powerful desire for material possessions and pleasures. Several of the Dreiser girls soon realized that men were a source of presents and possibly a way of escape from the bleak environment of the Dreiser home. They soon acquired bad reputations, which enraged their increasingly religious father. The boys left, one by one, as soon as they could find some means of escaping. Theodore was no exception. After a boyhood of moving from one dismal lodging to another, of scavenging for coal along the railroad tracks, of often having nothing but mush to eat, and of receiving only sporadic encouragement in a succession of schools (although he did become something of a voracious reader), Dreiser set out for Chicago when he was sixteen. He had six dollars in his pocket when he said goodby to his mother.

Like his own Sister Carrie, Dreiser found that Chicago was not in a welcoming mood when he got there. He had trouble finding work and finally had to take a job washing dishes. Though he soon found other employment, he failed at a succession of jobs before he was hired as a stock boy at five dollars a week by Hibbard, Spencer, Bartlett & Company, a wholesale hardware firm. Young and unsuited for any kind of manual work as he was, Dreiser had reason to be happy that he was able to be earning his living at all. But he was overcome with the hopelessness of his position—no education, no family resources to fall back upon, and little possibility of advancement within the huge and impersonal firm for which he worked. Ironically enough, Dreiser, the child of misfortune who was later to write so long and so sadly about the cruelties of fate, was called to the front office in the summer of 1889 to learn that for the first time in his life luck was on his side.

Waiting for him was Mildred Fielding, one of his former teachers, who had become principal of a Chicago high school. Dreiser, perhaps because of his brooding clumsiness, perhaps because of his strangeness, had stuck in her mind. She had tracked him down to make an incredible offer: she wanted to send him to Indiana University, and she would pay his costs. Through an event that would be unacceptable in his own novels, Dreiser found himself pulled from his squalid beginnings; a bright future seemed to be ahead.

But Indiana University was not Dreiser's world. He did not find himself intellectually stimulated; he made few friends; and he did not have the money to take much of a part in campus social life. Alone a great deal, he was depressed and restless. Once his freshman year was over, his formal education was at an end. Rejecting Miss Fielding's offer to finance him further, he returned to Chicago. College, it seemed, had turned out to be one more disappointment to him despite the glimpse it provided of a life he had never expected to experience at all. "In fact, now that I looked back on my college year," he later wrote, "I was irritated by the deprivations I had endured, the things in which I had not been included, the joys which many had had and which I had not."[1]

However, college had changed him, although not in the ordinary sense. It had not fired him with a desire for learning, but it had convinced him that he was just as intelligent as his generally well-to-do fellow students and that with work and some luck he might attain the material success for which he longed. So back he went to Chicago, where he aggressively began to seek his fortune, first as a real-estate salesman, then as a wagon driver for Munger's Laundry, and finally as a bill collector, before he realized that he was not going to get rich overnight. Trying to decide what to do next after he lost his bill collector's job (because of secretly borrowing against his account), for reasons that are obscure, Dreiser decided to become a newspaper reporter. Perhaps his wide reading (particularly in Tolstoy and Stevenson) suggested a career as a writer; or perhaps he saw newspapermen as people who get to meet the rich and famous. Whatever the motivation, Dreiser's decision to hang around the office of the Chicago *Daily Globe* until someone would give him a chance at being a reporter was the most important one he ever made. After two weeks of sitting in a chair and making himself conspicuous, Dreiser got his chance. The city editor had written a novel that was not selling well. If Dreiser would sell 120 copies of the novel on the streets, a probationary job on the newspaper staff would be arranged for him. It took Dreiser ten days, but he managed to sell the books, and the job was his.

Dreiser knew nothing about writing; and his natural style—long, cumbersome sentences—was unsuitable even for the journalism of the 1890s. But he had two things going for him: he was willing to rewrite and rewrite the simplest of his assignments; and he had a powerful curiosity that made him a good observer of people and events. In a surprisingly short time, he became an effective reporter, and within a year after going to work for the *Daily Globe*, he was offered a job at twenty dollars a week on the St. Louis *Globe-Democrat*, a much better paper. From then on, until he was able to depend on his novel-writing for support, Dreiser was a newspaperman and editor, working for the St. Louis *Republic*, the Cleveland *Leader*, the Pittsburgh *Dispatch*, the New York *World*, and later editing several magazines, including *Ev'ry Month*, *Broadway*, *The Bohemian*, and *The Delineator*.

Soon after becoming a newspaperman, Dreiser began to try his hand at other forms of writing. Through his acquaintance in St. Louis with two staff artists—Peter McCord and Richard Wood—Dreiser began to develop an interest in their "bohemian" way of life. His drift toward fiction writing was speeded when he became the drama critic for the *Globe-Democrat* and started to dream about becoming a dramatist. Under McCord's encouragement, Dreiser roughed out the plot of a comic opera, *Jeremiah I*, a preposterous tale about an Indiana farmer transported back to the Aztec empire. Dreiser was further impelled toward his eventual career by frustration over the restrictions placed upon what he could and could not report (the journalism code of the time prevented him from writing honestly about the grim events he saw daily as he made the rounds on his beats). In addition, he came under the influence of Arthur Henry, a young editor who had hired Dreiser for a few days' work on the Toledo *Blade*. An aspiring novelist himself, Arthur, who became for awhile one of Dreiser's closest friends, encouraged him to try writing fiction. He was invited to spend the summer of 1899 in the Henrys' house, where the two men set to work, each writing on a schedule, exchanging manuscripts, and criticizing one another's work. Dreiser sent some of his stories off for publication and eventually his first short story, "The Shining Slave Makers," was accepted by *Ainslee's*. Interestingly enough, the story concerned a young man who becomes a member of an ant colony and soon finds himself involved in the vicious warfare between two rival colonies.

Dreiser's short-story writing during that idyllic summer is of minor importance in comparison to another development. Henry was working on a novel and suggested that Dreiser do the same. Dreiser was uncertain, but as he said, "Finally I took out a piece of yellow paper and to please him wrote down a title at random—*Sister Carrie*. . . . My mind was a blank except for the name. I had no idea who or what she was to be. I have often thought there was something mystic about it, as if I were being used, like a medium."[2]

During the winter of 1899 and 1900 Dreiser continued to work on *Sister Carrie*, finishing it within seven months. After years of unconscious preparation, years spent observing and experiencing the cruelties of American life at the end of the nineteenth century, Dreiser hit upon the distinctive form that was to vary little throughout the rest of his life. As we shall see, *Sister Carrie* was not immediately successful, primarily because the publisher, Doubleday, belatedly decided to suppress it. However, the public may not have been ready for the novel in 1900, and *Sister Carrie* would have to wait for the recognition it eventually received (as would Dreiser himself). Nevertheless, Dreiser had found out what he could do; his main ideas were formulated, and his later books were inevitable. As

Alfred Kazin has written, "The very words he used, the dreaminess of his prose, the stilted but grim matter-of-fact of his method . . . all this seemed to say that it was not art he worked with but *knowledge*, some new and secret knowledge."[3]

Dreiser was superbly qualified to be the bearer of something new in 1900. At a time when the idea of gentility in literature, an idea generally associated with William Dean Howells, was beginning to wear thin, Dreiser's coarseness was a welcome change. Dreiser was an outsider, the first nonanglo-saxon, nonprotestant writer to become a major figure in American literature. He was also an uncouth, nervous, and somewhat mis-shapened man who, like the tycoons he was obsessed with, had a raging desire to get ahead. He was a fighter, often a bore, and many times he was cruel to people who had befriended and helped him. Yet he unquestionably knew things about American life that no other writer of his time quite did. He knew these things mainly because he was Theodore Dreiser.

Dreiser's personality has been the subject of much analysis. Ellen Moers has argued that there are two Dreisers (at least in terms of his work)—the Dreiser of the 1890s who was influenced by the same forces of naturalism that influenced Stephen Crane and Frank Norris, and the Dreiser of the post-World War I era who was influenced by Freudian psychology and the biological mechanism of the physiologist Jacques Loeb.[4] In his authoritative biography of Dreiser, W. A. Swanberg emphasizes the writer's moodiness, his manic-depressiveness, his tendency toward superstitution, and his lasting boorishness.[5] And far from being the least insightful portrait of all is provided by Dreiser's own autobiographical books: *Dawn* (1931), *A Book About Myself* (1922), *A Traveler at Forty* (1913), and *A*

Hoosier Holiday (1916). Although these works (listed according to their chronological sequence in Dreiser's life rather than dates of publication) vary considerably in mood, they present Dreiser in terms of the personality theory that most often comes up in his novels: "The mental and physical appetites of man alone explain him. He is, regardless of ideals or dreams or material equipment, an eating, savage animal, and in youth, and often in age, his greatest appetite, sex."[6] Dreiser's autobiographical writings are among the frankest ever put together, and they present a picture of a man who was capable of the coldest examination of his own life. Despite the haste with which they were written and the relatively little revising they went through, they also present a readable personal history of the 1890-1920 era.

But whatever approach is taken in interpreting Dreiser's personality, the facts are fascinating. His childhood can be seen as a classic oedipal plot, with Dreiser being torn between his love for his mother and his distaste for his father. Dreiser's relationship with his mother was probably the only tender one in his life; when she died in his arms in 1889, he fully experienced grief for the first and perhaps last time. He came from a large family, yet the only significant relationship he had with his brothers and sisters involved his older brother Paul, who became famous as a songwriter under the name of Paul Dresser. Paul, the author of "My Gal Sal," "On the Banks of the Wabash" (for which Dreiser wrote most of the lyrics), and "I Know It's True For My Mother Told Me So," was Dreiser's opposite in temperament; an outgoing, 300-pound compulsive entertainer, he was always willing to help his younger brother out. When Dreiser came to New York in 1894, Paul showed him around;

later Paul and his partners in the Howley, Haviland, & Company music publishing firm took him up on the proposition that he edit a magazine, *Ev'ry Month*, for them. But Dreiser never quite respected Paul, and occasionally, despite Paul's generosity, would not even acknowledge him when they met on the street. However, Dreiser and Paul did have one characteristic in common—sexual lives that needed no exaggeration.

From his adolescent encounter with a baker's girl in a Warsaw, Indiana, alley to his being thrown out of a California bordello while in his seventies for drinking and causing trouble, Dreiser's life is certainly support for his belief that in youth and in age man's greatest appetite is sexual. Dreiser went from one woman to the next, often carrying on affairs with several at once. Callously indifferent to the feelings of most of his women, he cheated on them (often openly), insulted them in front of friends, and was given to walking out abruptly and without explanation. He must be ranked as one of the all-time users of women, as a string of mistresses would undoubtedly testify.

In Dreiser's case it is no mere expression to say that a woman was not safe in the same room with him, whether other people were present or not. One can try to explain Dreiser's love life in terms of his feelings of inadequacy (for a long time as a young man he feared that he was impotent), uncertainty stemming from his appearance (he was tall, thin, and had a permanent cast in one eye), or simply that he knew no other way to gain affection. But the best and most direct explanation is that he thought of himself in the same mechanistically biological way that he thought of the characters in his novels. Dreiser considered himself driven by the biological and environmental factors he called "chemisms," a term he never defined exactly but which implies a strict physical and "scientific" view of human behavior. Some have mistakenly suggested that he had a straightforward theory of brain chemistry, but actually Dreiser believed that the forces working on, in, and through all of us are part of some sort of incredible, cosmic stew. He was inclined to think that chemisms had led him into his first marriage and then had led him out of it and into the lengthy involvement that eventually resulted in his second marriage (with dozens of other involvements along the way). One need not go too far into Dreiser's theory of chemisms, however, to realize that it was a convenient way to explain actions that would otherwise be termed cruel or irresponsible. As a theory, it only goes part of the way in explaining the character development that takes place in Dreiser's novels—or the development of Dreiser's own personality for that matter.

Chemisms or not, in 1898 Dreiser married Sallie White, a Missouri schoolteacher he had met while working in St. Louis; he separated permanently from her in 1909, but never earnestly sought a divorce. Even after Sallie died in 1942, he waited until 1944 before marrying Helen Richardson, his cousin, whom he had met in 1919 and with whom he lived off-and-on thereafter. The two women were near opposites. Sallie, nicknamed "Jug," was a country girl whose one claim to sophistication was a trip to the Chicago World's Fair. Helen was a beautiful woman who had a promising career as a movie actress. That Dreiser at times was happy with each of these women is another indication of the essential duality of his personality.

This duality can be seen in several ways. It is evident in the simple contrast between the two women

—Sallie offering Dreiser midwestern virtue and Helen offering Hollywood glamor. It figures, as Swanberg emphasizes, in Dreiser's hesitations on the matter of marriage itself: "True, he loved Jug—or did he? He could never make up his mind because he was forever weighing the factors: sincere affection and sincere doubts, his desire to have the advantages of both estates and the disadvantages of neither, the pleasure of wifely admiration and home cooking plus the perfect freedom of the artist, philosopher and rake."[7] And it can be seen in the nervous breakdown he suffered in 1902.

Depressed by the virtual suppression of *Sister Carrie*, unable to work out editorial problems in his next novel, *Jennie Gerhardt*, experiencing financial problems, increasingly unhappy in his marriage, and suffering from neurasthenia, he wound up in an eight-by-six, $1.25-a-week room in Brooklyn unable to work, convinced he was going crazy, and contemplating suicide. At the lowest point in this slide toward despair, Dreiser saw himself dividing into two persons, "one a tall, selfish individual, the other a silent philosopher who watched his struggles with calm detachment."[8] The "first" Dreiser is, of course, the one who pursued every woman he met, the Dreiser who wanted to take everything he could take—Dreiser as he actually lived. The other Dreiser, philosophic in his detachment, is the Dreiser who comes through in the often compassionate point-of-view in his novels.

Fortunately for Dreiser, he was not allowed to sink to the point where his double nature would split permanently. One day, while walking up Broadway, he ran into his brother Paul. Dreiser had been too proud to seek help, but once Paul saw the condition his younger brother was in, he took immediate action.

Paul arranged for Dreiser to spend six weeks at a
Westchester recuperation center run by William Muldoon, a former champion wrestler. Thanks to Muldoon's vigorous regimen of exercise combined with a
healthful diet, Dreiser got himself back together. After
leaving Muldoon's on June 2, Dreiser found work as
a laborer at New York Central's Spuyten Duyvil shop
on the Hudson. By Christmas, the physical therapy
had done its job and Dreiser felt strong enough to
begin writing again. Despite a lifelong tendency toward
depression, Dreiser's major crisis was past.

But Dreiser's contradictory frame of mind was a
constant factor in his career, especially in his leftward
drift after the 1920s. From the beginning, as a writer
Dreiser expressed a distrust of American capitalism, a
distrust obviously stemming from the misfortunes
brought on the Dreiser family by the destruction of
John Dreiser's woolen mill. By 1931, when he led a
communist-sponsored committee (one of whose members was John Dos Passos) to investigate the struggle
in Harlan County, Kentucky, between the coal miners
and operators over unionization, Dreiser's hostility toward capitalism found expression in action; it had
already been expressed through print in the book that
resulted from his 1927-28 visit to Russia (at the invitation of the Soviet government), *Dreiser Looks at
Russia.*

In 1932 Dreiser applied for membership in the
American Communist Party but was gently refused by
party head Earl Browder, who did not believe that
Dreiser's orientation was sufficiently Marxist. In 1945
he again applied for membership and this time was
accepted; but Dreiser never did abandon his view of
life as a jungle. Even more heretical, as he became

increasingly involved in communist programs, he steadily invested much of his earnings in real estate, thus
becoming a secret capitalist himself.

Many of Dreiser's peculiarities as well as his
strengths can be understood more broadly in terms of
the era in which he grew to maturity. This is particularly true of the period up to 1900, during which he
was influenced greatly by post-Darwinian evolutionary
thinking, a point of view that is effectively stated in
Herbert Spencer's phrase about the "survival of the
fittest." This phase was used to justify American ex-
pansionism (especially the Spanish-American War),
the exploitation of workers, and even the misfortunes
of Dreiser's father. So while Dreiser was being nur-
tured in the Catholicism of his parents, he was growing up in a society that was increasingly and mani-
festly being organized around an idea of jungle warfare.

In 1894, when he was working in Pittsburgh,
Dreiser encountered the evolutionary outlook head-on
in Thomas Huxley's *Science and Hebrew Tradition*
and *Science and Christian Tradition* and Spencer's
First Principles. Huxley effectively devastated Dreiser's
belief in his childhood religion, and Spencer convinced
him that man is merely a matter of chemical reactions,
a mechanism in the control of an Unknown Cause.
Dreiser said he was nearly destroyed by reading Spencer, who, as he emphasized, "took every shred of
belief away from me; showed me that I was a chemical
atom in a whirl of unknown forces. . ."[9] Although
Dreiser used Spencer's ideas to justify his later often
cruel and selfish actions, Spencer, as well as Huxley,
embittered him. It is as if he resented forevermore
having to give up comforting beliefs, to face the reality
of a world that offered only excuses for viciousness.

Unlike his older contemporary William James, Dreiser found little to support the validity of religious belief in an evolutionary universe, although in his later work, particularly *The Bulwark*, there is movement toward a kind of religious consciousness.

Nevertheless, true to his contradictory nature, he was not unable to find some cause for optimism, some belief in the possibilities of social progress despite his grim acceptance of Huxley and Spencer. This is because Dreiser is also a product of the Progressive Era, the period roughly beginning with Theodore Roosevelt's election in 1901 and closing with the United States' entry into World War I in 1917. Progressivism in its most obvious sense was the reaction to the cruelties engendered by the belief in unbridled individualism that was a part of nineteenth-century evolutionism and industrialism. The Gilded Age, with its robber-barons, its Jay Goulds and John D. Rockefellers, its economic panics, its abusive working conditions, its exploitation of immigrant peoples, and its pervasive amorality, taught American reformers a hard lesson: in an urbanized, manufacturing society, unrestrained individualism meant societal destruction. Through the work of such writers as Ida Tarbell, Lincoln Steffens, Samuel Hopkins Adams, Burton Henrick, and other "muckrakers," political and economic corruption of an incredible variety was exposed, forcing Theodore Roosevelt to call for action in restraint of the tooth-and-claw ethic that had come to dominate American life. Simple reforms were not enough for many of the advocates of change, however, and some, such as Upton Sinclair and later Steffens began to argue that a change to socialism, perhaps even a revolution, was the only answer.

Dreiser was directly influenced by the Progressive

mood in several ways. First, he was fascinated by the image of the tycoon, particularly that of Charles T. Yerkes, the Chicago streetcar magnate who became the basis for Dreiser's Cowperwood trilogy: *The Financier*, (1912), *The Titan* (1914), and *The Stoic* (1947). One of the major conflicts in the trilogy involves Cowperwood's reaction to the anti-superman policies that came out of the post-1900 reforms. Second, Dreiser lived in Greenwich Village in its heyday, when it was the center of the reform movement. Low rents and the independent atmosphere had attracted writers and radicals to the Village, and by 1912 some of these intellectuals had banded together in the Liberal Club, and the publication of the *Masses*, under the editorship of Max Eastman and Floyd Dell had begun. In 1914 Dreiser and his current mistress, Kirah Markham, moved into two first-floor rooms at No. 7, 165 West Tenth Street, where he lived for the next five years, variously encountering Dell, Steffens, Eastman, John Reed, Big Bill Haywood, and other leftists. While Dreiser remained pessimistic about the possibility of improving the human condition, living amid all this leftist fervor undoubtedly influenced him in his eventual belief that communism might offer at least some amelioration. The endings of *Sister Carrie, Jennie Gerhardt*, and even the much later *An American Tragedy* are dismal, but the documentation of misery in these books has an air of exposé to it that is reminiscent of Tarbell, Steffens, and Sinclair.

Several other relationships between Dreiser and the Progressive Era are often overlooked. For one thing, by 1910 or 1912 Dreiser's growing reputation as a literary rebel put him in the forefront of the many writers who thought of themselves in the same way. And for another thing, one of the dominant themes of

the times, the liberation of the American woman, became a central theme in Dreiser's work. This was especially true of his portrait of Jennie Gerhardt, but it
was also true of the sketches published in 1929 as
A Gallery of Women.

However, what made Dreiser the foremost figure
in the new American literature of the pre-1920 period
was his battle against censorship, a battle that began
with the publication of *Sister Carrie,* culminated in
the uproar evoked by *The "Genius"* in 1916, and continued off-and-on throughout Dreiser's life. Given the
repressive publishing code and the popular taste of the
day, it is not surprising that *Sister Carrie* with its story
of vice—at least insofar as Carrie herself is concerned
—being rewarded instead of punished, should have
gotten Dreiser into trouble. The novel was accepted
for publication by Doubleday, Page & Co., primarily
on the urging of novelist Frank Norris, himself a pro-
ponent of realism, who was working for Doubleday as
an editor. Frank Doubleday, the head of the publishing house, was in England at the time. When he returned, he took the novel home and gave it to his
wife to read. Mrs. Doubleday, understandably enough,
was shocked.

Her attitudes were those shared by many reason-
ably sophisticated readers, and are reflected in William
Dean Howells's attempt in *Criticism and Fiction*
(1891) at defining modern literary standards. While
endorsing realism in the sense of truthfulness to detail,
Howells maintained that art should teach rather than
amuse—that it should, more directly, inculcate morality. This, he argued, could perhaps be best achieved
by concentrating on the more positive, happier aspects
of life, which are, as he saw it, the more American.

Sister Carrie hardly fit into this mold. Mrs. Double-

day advised her husband to somehow get out of his
contract with Dreiser, and he decided to do as she
said. But Dreiser was adamant and resisted every com-
promise Doubleday suggested. The company finally
went along with its obligations, but Doubleday resisted distributing the book, even though Norris managed to get copies to some reviewers. Nonetheless, the
novel was effectively suppressed in America until it
was reissued by B. W. Dodge & Co. in 1907.

The attack on *The "Genius,"* a story much more
openly erotic in its descriptions, was more widespread
and above-board than Frank Doubleday's autocratic
stifling of *Sister Carrie.* Dreiser's nemesis in 1916 was
the New York Society for the Suppression of Vice, an
organization that had worked to expurgate, condemn,
and even ban Rabelais, Shakespeare, Balzac, Zola,
Hardy, and others. John S. Sumner, successor to the
Society's famous founder, Anthony Comstock, succeeded in frightening the publisher, the John Lane
Co., into withdrawing the novel. The novelist and his
friend H. L. Mencken went to work to save the book.
Dreiser first shipped the plates of *The "Genius"* out
of state to offset the possibility of their being destroyed. In August 1916 support was gained from the
Authors League of America, which stated that the
book was not obscene. Mencken gained further support
for Dreiser by obtaining 478 signatures in defense of
The "Genius" from other writers; those signing included Ezra Pound, Sherwood Anderson, Ida Tarbell,
Arnold Bennett, and H. G. Wells, although surprisingly enough, some important literary figures, most
notably the early realist Hamlin Garland, refused to
sign.

Dreiser continued the battle by bringing suit
against the publishers. The case was heard by the

Appellate Division of the Supreme Court in May, 1918: unfortunately the five judges ruled against Dreiser, and *The "Genius"* remained off the market until five years later, when it was issued by Horace Liveright. Dreiser lost, but the reality of the threat to freedom of expression was brought home to American writers, readers, and critics (previous legal suppressions had involved either foreign or long-deceased authors). In just a few years, much of what Dreiser had battled for was to be achieved. In 1922, for example, James Branch Cabell was absolved of obscenity eighteen months after the New York Society for the Suppression of Vice had forced withdrawal of his *Jurgen*, a comic, pseudomedieval novel containing some fairly graphic sexual passages. In subsequent trials involving Joyce's *Ulysses*, Lawrence's *Lady Chatterley's Lover*, and even such books as *Fanny Hill*, Dreiser's example remained an object lesson.

Again and again, Dreiser spoke out in defense of the artist's right to be heard. One of his most important actions of this sort developed, surprisingly enough, out of his involvement with Hollywood, which is a story in itself.

Dreiser first went to the movie capital in 1919 with Helen, who secured minor roles in such films as *The Flame of Youth* and Valentino's *The Four Horsemen of the Apocalypse*. They lived for a time in a bungalow on Sunset Boulevard and began to speculate in Hollywood property, buying several lots in the Montrose section and then selling them at a profit. But Dreiser's interest in the film colony also took a more literary turn in two essays he published during 1921, "Hollywood Now" in *McCall's* and "Hollywood, Its

Morals and Mannerisms" for *Shadowland*, a film magazine. His attack on money-grubbing among those associated with the film industry was later to seem somewhat ironic when he began to haggle with Paramount's Famous Players over the screen rights to *An American Tragedy*. This series of negotiations, threats, and counterthreats eventually led to an important clarification of the relationship between writers and producers.

From the very start, the screen adaptation of *An American Tragedy* ran into trouble. In mid-March of 1926, a luncheon conference at the Ritz in New York was arranged to discuss the financial arrangements that were to precede work on the film. Dreiser and his publisher, Horace Liveright, met with Paramount representatives. Dreiser had previously mentioned his price —$100,000, a figure that seemed, for the times, outrageous. But he insisted on sticking to it. Liveright somehow was led to expect a 30 percent cut, and it was with this share in mind that he proposed the $100,000 deal to the Paramount officials. He then left the table so that Dreiser and the contract men could negotiate. When Liveright returned, he learned that they had settled on $90,000. Liveright did not object, but mentioned that he still expected his 30 percent. Dreiser told him that he would get 10 percent, and denied having made a promise of a 70–30 split. Liveright called him a liar, and then the real action began.

Dreiser jumped up and raised his fists, demanding that Liveright stand and fight. Since the novelist outweighed the publisher by some seventy pounds, Liveright chose to remain where he was. Dreiser reached down, grabbed a coffee cup, and splashed coffee in Liveright's face, thereby ending negotiations for that day. A few days later, however, matters were settled at the $90,000 figure, with Liveright still getting only 10 percent.

Neither Dreiser's troubles nor his suspicions were ended with the signing of the contract. First there was a delay of several years as Paramount tried to decide what to do with what was, after all, a controversial property. Nothing at all was done until Russian film director Sergei Eisenstein went to Hollywood in 1930. Paramount interested him in adapting the book, and Eisenstein, along with Ivor Montagu, prepared a script for a million-dollar, twelve-reel production. Eisenstein visited Dreiser at Iroki, Dreiser's country retreat in upstate New York, and talked about *An American Tragedy* as an indictment of the United States. Dreiser apparently was much impressed with the ideas of Eisenstein and Montagu. The resulting script was a version concentrating upon Clyde's innocence and the corruption of American society. Paramount backed down, fearing the consequences of putting out so radical a film in a time of economic crisis. (The film company may also have been frightened by the fact that Dreiser's leftist pronouncements were becoming louder and more frequent.)

Paramount consequently settled, in December 1930, on a shorter script by Samuel Hoffenstein with Josef von Sternberg as director. Having signed an additional $55,000 contract for the sound rights, Dreiser, feeling flush, left early the next year for Havana, his exact address a secret. The Hoffenstein script was completed quickly, and efforts were made to find Dreiser. When he finally turned up, production was about to begin, and he had not exercised his option to comment on the script. When Dreiser at last got around to reading it, he was outraged by the concentration on the trial scenes at the expense of social criticism. Dreiser wrote to Hoffenstein and told him that the script was an insult to the book's scope and emotional background. Dreiser's mood was worsened by Sternberg's off-hand comment to a newspaper reporter that Dreiser was washed-up as a writer; this remark confirmed what the novelist had suspected—that Sternberg had little sympathy for his book. Dreiser accordingly proposed that he and a friend prepare a revised script and that Sternberg be fired as director. He threatened legal action if Paramount went ahead with the production and associated his name with it.

Dreiser's objections, as Swanberg points out,[10] were disturbing to the Hollywood moguls. He was in effect insisting on thinking of movies as essentially art, not entertainment. Hollywood producers had vulgarized so many novels and stories that writers had for the most part come to regard cheap and erroneous versions of their work as no more than what was to be expected. Dreiser would entertain no such expectations.

Eventually he set up an incredible apparatus to judge the finished Paramount product. An eighteen-member committee, including, among others, writers and critics such as George Jean Nathan, Carl Van Doren, Floyd Dell, Ernest Boyd, and Burton Rascoe, was formed to see the film and pinpoint any violation of Dreiser's masterpiece. Dreiser also added a subjury of twenty or so, among whom were Herbert Bayard Swope and Alexander Woollcott. Paramount agreed to give an advance showing in New York on June 15, 1931, and Dreiser's "jurors" saw Phillips Holmes as Clyde, Sylvia Sidney as Roberta, and Frances Dee as Sondra. Some of those at the preview realized the difficulties inherent in making a movie out of *An*

American Tragedy, but most readily testified that the
film was full of weaknesses and that the spirit of
Dreiser's book had been all but smothered. Dreiser
himself agreed with such condemnations and proceeded to obtain an injunction. Paramount was forced
to show cause that it ought not to be stopped from
distributing the film.

The case was heard the following July 22 in
White Plains, New York. Dreiser found the argument
running against him from the very beginning and was
soon moved to angry outbursts when the Paramount
attorney accused him of stealing the plot line of *An
American Tragedy* from the newspapers. Several times
the judge had to warn him to keep quiet. The decision
ultimately went against Dreiser, but he had made
Hollywood more aware of authors' rights and, once
again, had fought a battle that would benefit other
writers.

Nor was Dreiser through with Paramount, despite
his suit against them; a year later, in 1932, Paramount
paid him $25,000 for *Jennie Gerhardt*. Soon trouble
was developing again. A news story cited a Paramount
official, B. P. Schulberg, as saying that the company
made certain this time that Dreiser had no control
over the script and that if Dreiser did not like the
film version he was powerless to object. Dreiser's angry
rebuttal was headlined in *Variety*, but Schulberg was
right; Dreiser found out that he could indeed do
nothing. Oddly enough, when Dreiser saw the film
starring Sylvia Sidney as Jennie, he was pleased, and
graciously wired his praise to Schulberg.

Sister Carrie, by the way, was sold to RKO in the
fall of 1940 for $40,000. It was produced in 1951 with
Jennifer Jones and Laurence Olivier in lead roles.

An American Tragedy had to wait until that same

year before Paramount finally made a successful version of it, unfortunately under another title, A *Place
in the Sun*. The casting turned out to be nearly exact,
with Montgomery Clift as Clyde, Shelley Winters as
an evocative Roberta, and Elizabeth Taylor as Sondra.
Although George Stevens does not present Clyde's
guilt with sufficient ambiguity, the movie comes across
as strikingly compassionate. Dreiser would undoubtedly
have found A *Place in the Sun* insufficiently polemical,
but perhaps he would have agreed that the sense of
loss that emerges in the final scenes compares faith-
fully with the kind of feeling that is behind a similar
mood in his fiction. One would hope, at any rate, that
the successful remake of An *American Tragedy* was
at least partly a result of Dreiser's insistence, twenty
years earlier, on an author's right to demand an honest
interpretation of his book. And, of course, that the
movie could be made as frankly as it was in 1951 is
more than a little due to the campaign for freedom
of expression that Dreiser had waged over a half century before for the right to publish *Sister Carrie*.

One of the ironies in Dreiser's struggle for literary
freedom is that during the years when copies of *Sister
Carrie* were locked up in the basement of Doubleday's
Union Square plant, Dreiser rose to the editorship of
The Delineator, one of the silliest and most syrupy
publications in the history of women's magazines. *The
Delineator* was owned by Butterick's, the leading publisher of dress patterns. Here is Dreiser's own statement on *The Delineator*'s editorial policy: "We cannot
admit stories which deal with false or immoral relations, or which point a false moral, or which deal with
things degrading, such as drunkenness. I am personally
opposed in this magazine to stories which have an
element of horror in them or which are disgusting in

their realism and fidelity to life."[11] Dreiser's work for
The Delineator can be defended by arguing that he
could not turn down the salary Butterick's was willing
to pay (when he was fired in 1910 because of a poten-
tial scandal involving a young girl with whom he had
fallen in love, he was making $10,000 a year); but, as
Swanberg writes, Dreiser's being hired by Butterick's
"was the literary joke of the century—Dreiser the
apostate, the libertine, the enemy of prudery, the
fighter for realism, the author of *Sister Carrie*, becoming the high arbiter of dainty stories for dainty women,
the iconoclast turned hymnsinger."[12] But then the
element of Progressive compassion that was so much
a part of Dreiser's makeup was not without some relationship to his duties on *The Delineator*.

Yet Dreiser's work for Butterick's was not inconsistent with his other view of life, no matter how
inconsistent it might in some ways seem. Life is a
jungle and a man must survive however he can; and
that is just what Dreiser did by taking *The Delineator*
job. However one might want to fault Dreiser for lack
of character in so many respects, one is nonetheless
struck by the coolly realistic way he went about living
his life. He was a man of contradictions; often cruel
to others, he was perhaps needlessly cruel to himself.
But he confronted life in a manner that few of his
contemporaries were willing to do, and in most instances he lived in accordance with his artistic credo:
"For I take no meaning from life other than the picture it presents to the eye—the pleasure and pain it
gives to the body."[13] But, as we shall see, he was not as
hard-boiled as all that.

2

Dreiser's Women

Apparently each of us—certainly the most of us—as Nietzsche points out, seems to draw a certain kind of success or disaster, about as plants draw a certain kind of insect or a given type of tree the lightning. We have, or are, a fate in ourselves.

—*A Gallery of Women*

*S*ister *Carrie* is one of the most inexplicable of books not because it is difficult to understand, but because of all the questions concerning how it came to be what it is and how it came to be at all. Consider the odds. A shambling man of nearly thirty with a marginal education and no clear conception of what was happening in the literary world sits down at his friend's urging, scrawls a title on the top of a sheet of paper, and eventually writes the novel with which, it may be argued, American literature moves into the twentieth century (the book was first published in 1900). Dreiser's *Sister Carrie* created a scandal (somewhat overexaggerated, as we shall see) when it appeared, but the very fact that Dreiser wrote it has become even more of a scandal. It is not difficult, given the personality and background of, say, a Henry James or even a Sinclair Lewis, to understand their kinds of accomplishment; but to many, that Dreiser could write novels at all is implausible. And what is perhaps more difficult to accept is that Dreiser, the notorious exploiter of women, could devote his first two books to the development of sympathetic and sensitive portraits of women. One answer to all of this is, of course, that Dreiser's novels are like the man who wrote them: several sided, contradictory, and large.

There is in Dreiser some of the same unconscious genius that is attributed to Dickens, and this in itself goes a long way toward explaining the inexplicableness of Dreiser's achievement, incredibly pat though this answer may be. This unconscious genius is evident from the very first sentence of *Sister Carrie* in Dreiser's casual use of symbols that at once establish the elements of the story: "When Caroline Meeber boarded the afternoon train for Chicago, her total outfit consisted of a small trunk, a cheap imitation alligator-skin satchel, a small lunch in a paper box, and a yellow snap purse, containing her ticket, a scrap of paper with her sister's address on Van Buren Street, and four dollars in money."[1] As this first sentence indicates, Carrie is a fate unto herself, boarding the train (that simultaneous image of free will and determinism) with her cheap luggage (a sign of her poverty and an indication of what she is escaping from), her sister's address on a scrap of paper (easily lost, and, of course, her sister's apartment is in a scrap heap of a building), and only four dollars in cash (again and again what happens to Carrie is a function of certain sums of money). Dreiser also mentions that Carrie is going to Chicago, the city that almost becomes a character itself in the novel and to which Dreiser returns again in his later books whenever he wants to evoke the beauty and terror of the American industrial state and its impact on the hopeful mind.

Carrie, given what she is in Dreiser's first mention of her, begins to draw a certain kind of success or disaster about her. "She was eighteen years of age, bright, timid, and full of the illusion of ignorance and youth,"[2] and what else is to be expected but that she soon catches the eye of a traveling salesman? Charles Drouet is, as Dreiser puts it, a "masher," a type lifted from the popular literature of the day, specifically from the writing of the then-famous Chicago humorist George Ade. Drouet's clothing (white-and-pink-striped shirt, patterned suit of brown wool, linen cuffs with cat's-eyes buttons, tan shoes, and a gray fedora), his manner of speaking, and his whole way of coming-on are directed toward eliciting the admiration of girls who, like Carrie, are susceptible and young. Before many miles have passed Drouet has obtained Carrie's Chicago address as well as permission to call on her

the following Monday night. As any reader of the
thousands of melodramatic tales that were written in
the latter half of the nineteenth century would know
at this point, Carrie's future does not look promising;
and before the first chapter is over, Carrie's seduction
by Drouet seems inevitable. It is here, however, that
Dreiser's moral ambiguity takes over: whether what
happens to Carrie is indeed bad depends on the reader's
point-of-view.

With the meeting of Carrie and Drouet the first
of several ironies that were especially offensive to many
of Dreiser's early detractors begins. Carrie leaves Drouet
at the train station and goes to live with her sister and
brother-in-law in a dreary flat. She must find work, so
the next day she begins the frightening and discourag-
ing round of manufacturing houses and department
stores. Only after hours of going from place-to-place
does she get a job running a punch machine in a shoe
factory at $4.50 a week. As bad as the working condi-
tions are, as disheartening as it is to pay all but fifty
cents of her weekly earnings for room and board,
Carrie struggles on respectably. She discourages Drouet's
Monday-night visit (mainly, it should be pointed out,
because she is ashamed to receive him in her sister's
apartment) and works steadily until one fall day she
falls sick. Because she cannot go to work for a few
days, she loses her job. When she recovers, she is once
more forced to look for employment, this time with
winter coming on and with little recollection of the
hopefulness she had felt upon arriving in Chicago.

By chance, Drouet sees her on the street; he takes
her out for dinner; he presses two ten-dollar bills on
her; soon he has set her up in a room, then an apartment, and Carrie has fallen. "Oh," moans Carrie's
sister when she realizes why Carrie left, "poor Sister

Carrie!"[3] But through her fall, Carrie has risen, and she will not act the part of the ruined girl. Her life through the rest of the novel is "represented by an especially upward spiral."[4] She meets a better man than Drouet, eventually becomes a music-hall actress, and ends as an independent woman.

The better man she meets is G. W. Hurstwood, the manager of Fitzgerald and Moy's saloon, one of Drouet's hangouts. Hurstwood dresses with more sophistication than Drouet, has better manners, and is to Carrie clearly superior. Just as Carrie at the start of the novel is a stereotype of the innocent country girl on the way to the wicked city, Hurstwood is representative of the successful middle-class American man of the type Sinclair Lewis would later caricature in *Babbitt*—respected, prosperous, married, and a father. But he is inwardly discontented. His wife is shrewish, his children are spoiled, and he is aging. It is inevitable that he be drawn to a girl like Carrie.

Dreiser invites the reader to sense Hurstwood's restlessness, encourages us to cheer him on as he gets involved with Carrie, steals money from his employer, and runs off with her. After all, Dreiser has indicated that Carrie is going to get away with abandoning respectability. But ironically Hurstwood does not get away with it. His career, once he decides to chuck everything for love, is a downward spiral. Carrie, because of what she is, draws a certain kind of success; Hurstwood, in turn, because of what he is, draws a certain kind of disaster.

Much has been made of Dreiser's determinism, his emphasis on fate, environment, the influence of outside forces on the protagonists of his novels. But the sense of inevitability that runs through his fiction derives more from the kind of characterization that is basic to his technique. One of Dreiser's powers is his ability to lay the groundwork for a character's development in a few sentences. Drouet is described as follows: "He bobbed about among men, a veritable bundle of enthusiasm—no power worthy the name of intellect, no thought worthy the adjective noble, no feelings long continued in one strain."[5] Carrie's personality is outlined less concisely but just as tellingly: "Nature has taught the beasts of the field to fly when some unheralded danger threatens. She has put into the small unwise head of the chipmunk the untutored fear of poisons. 'He keepeth his creatures whole,' is not written of beasts alone. Carrie was unwise, and, therefore, like the sheep in its unwisdom, strong in feeling."[6] From these descriptions it is possible to predict and trace the development of two of the three major figures in the novel. It is evident that there will be no tragedy associated with Drouet, for he is not noble and is not capable of containing the feelings necessary to a tragic hero. Nor will there be tragedy for Carrie—no more than there could be tragedy for the chipmunk; instinct and tragedy are not compatible. As the novel evolves, Drouet stays as buoyant as ever and Carrie is instinctively carried from Columbia City to Chicago to New York—to success. But the characterization Dreiser gives to his third major protagonist, G. W. Hurstwood, with whom tragedy *is* associated, is not so simple, and his development is not so easy to predict or trace.

Hurstwood has long been seen by many commentators as the most interesting character in *Sister Carrie*. This is partly because Carrie is hardly developed as a person; she says little that is memorable, although there is an unconscious calculating quality about her that, as both Drouet and Hurstwood learn, make her somewhat dangerous. If she is not quite a *femme fatale*, she is far more than the ordinary "other woman." But, as F. O. Matthiessen emphasizes in his study of Dreiser, the novelist's "most serious inadequacy in presenting his heroine is not what Mrs. Doubleday thought —that Carrie is too unconventional—but, that she is not unconventional enough."[7] Hurstwood is also conventional, but he is presented with considerably more complexity than Carrie. "Above all else," James T. Farrell wrote in 1945, "the reason why *Sister Carrie*, to this day, remains so meaningful, so moving and so compelling a novel is Dreiser's portrait of Hurstwood. In Hurstwood, type and individuality merge so well that they are practically indistinguishable."[8] Hurstwood is at once a representative man and a unique creation whose decline and fall holds a strange fascination over the reader. This is in large part simply due to the unhurried and detailed account Dreiser gives us to him.

Hurstwood is the only character in *Sister Carrie* to be treated in scientific—that is, casebook—fashion. Nothing is said of Drouet's home life and very little of his past. Carrie's life in Columbia City is virtually ignored. However, Hurstwood's past and home life receive fairly extensive elaboration. His rise from bartender to manager is outlined, the change that occurs in his family as he becomes more affluent receives attention, emphasis is given his gradual alienation from his family, and even his financial status is disclosed (forty thousand in property, all in his wife's name). It is against this completely detailed background that Hurstwood's relationship to Carrie is seen. Such delineation is necessary if Hurstwood is to be an expression of one aspect of Dreiser's determinism and of his partial acceptance of free will.

Within the first paragraph of chapter eight, Dreiser comes as close to a summation of Hurstwood's condition as he does anywhere else in the novel: "We see man far removed from the lairs of the jungles, his innate instincts dulled by too near an approach to free-will, his free-will not sufficiently developed to replace his instincts and afford him perfect guidance. He is becoming too wise to hearken always to instincts and desires; he is still too weak to always prevail against them."[9] In the initial elaboration given Hurstwood's character, his instincts for survival are at least superficially evident. He senses that there can be no complication in his home life if he is to keep his comfortable job; his employers want no scandals. Hurstwood does not have to think about the necessity for dignified conduct: "He knew the need of it".[10] But, he becomes too wise to heed his instincts. He begins to think that his life can be made more complete, that he can achieve greater happiness, if he has Carrie. And he is too weak to prevail against his desires. Consequently, he exercises what seems to be free will in pursuing Carrie and attempting to secure some sort of arrangement whereby he can maintain her and his family at the same time. But he fails to exercise the necessary caution; Mrs. Hurstwood learns that her husband has been seeing another woman, and utilizes the opportunity to sue for divorce. Hurstwood again reverts to his will in an effort to escape from the embarassing situation his wife's action throws him into. But he fails when he resorts to robbery, he fails to successfully invest his money in New York, and he fails to hold Carrie. In his failures it is evident that

Hurstwood's free will is not sufficiently developed to replace his instincts in guiding action.

The conflict between free will and determinism reaches its symbolic height in *Sister Carrie* when Hurstwood, depressed by his wife's divorce action and desperate for a solution to his problems, discovers that the cashier at Fitzgerald and Moy's has forgotten to twist the safe dial and that consequently the lock is not sprung. This is one of Dreiser's most famous scenes and undoubtedly one of his most effective in suggesting the mystery that lies behind crisis behavior, a mystery that is central in much of Dreiser's later writing, especially *An American Tragedy*.

Hurstwood is all alone in the office, the saloon has been closed, and it is his responsibility to see that everything is secured for the night. Only the owners and the cashier know the combination to the safe, and it has never been left open before. Hurstwood, as is his custom, tests the safe door. It opens. The money is there, bills in parcels of a thousand. He shuts the door, opens it again, takes the money out, thinks he hears somebody, puts the money back, takes it out again, then returns it, apparently for the final time.

But he begins to doubt that he has replaced the money in the proper cash drawers. He takes the money out to rearrange it, and while he is holding the cash in his hands, the lock on the safe door somehow clicks. Now he has to go through with what he had contemplated doing—he must find Carrie and get out of the country. But the overwhelming question remains: did Hurstwood willingly steal the money and make his fateful decision, or was his hand forced by the clicking of the lock? Hurstwood's anguished deliberation only intensifies the question. Is he capable of exercising free will or is he still dominated by instinct, in this case his instinctive fear of being caught? "The dullest specimen of humanity, when drawn by desire toward evil, is recalled by a sense of right, which is proportionate in power and strength to his evil tendency," Dreiser comments. "We must remember that it may not be a knowledge of right, for no knowledge of right is predicated of the animal's instinctive recoil at evil. Men are still led by instinct before they are regulated by knowledge."[11]

Once the act is done, Hurstwood is decisive. But he has not thought things out very well. Fitzgerald and Moy put a detective on his trail, and Hurstwood realizes the full consequences of what he has done. His will begins to falter; in Montreal, he decides to return all but $1,300 of the money, instead of following through on his original plan to slip into New York with all of his fortune. He and Carrie are married (Hurstwood takes the false name of Wheeler—ironic because he has shown that he is anything but a wheeler and dealer). When they reach New York City, they get along for awhile; but Hurstwood has not preserved enough capital to ensure his survival. He invests in a saloon partnership, but is left with only $700 when the building in which he has leased the saloon is sold to make room for another structure. Winter arrives, a time of massive unemployment. His money dwindles. He and Carrie move to smaller quarters and it is soon evident that Hurstwood cannot provide for her.

On the strength of the amateur acting she did while in Chicago, Carrie gets a job as a chorus girl. Again, as in letting herself be picked up by Drouet, she is doing the "wrong" thing. But once more, the step toward ruin is a step toward success for Carrie. Meanwhile Hurstwood's deterioration is slowly documented by Dreiser, right down to the moment when,

abandoned by Carrie and weakened by beggary, Hurstwood tucks his coat along the crack under the door
in a fifteen-cent flophouse room, turns on the gas, and
asks, "What's the use?"[12] And when we think back
to the event that precipitated all of this, the springing
of the safe-door lock, we are led to echo the question.
In Hurstwood's inability to sustain the choice that
is forced upon him is the essence of his tragedy. In
the paralysis of will that afflicts him in the theft scene,
we see that his free will is indeed not sufficiently developed to replace his instincts; and we also realize
that Hurstwood, with all of the self-assurance that so
impresses Carrie, is not so far removed from the lair
of the jungle.

The development Dreiser gives Hurstwood is one
of the best and fullest treatments of deterministic
philosophy to be found anywhere in his work. Through
Hurstwood, more than through any other character in
Sister Carrie, Dreiser dramatizes "man's utmost help-
lessness when strength of will is most needed" and
creates thereby "a sense of the superb irony of the fate
of man"[13]—free to choose, yet not free to choose, because before the final choice is made the lock clicks.

This emphasis on the denial of freedom, along
with Dreiser's quasi-scientific and quasi-philosophic
explanation of it in the many asides that serve as
commentary on the narration, has given Dreiser the
reputation of being one of the first naturalists in
American literature. There are varying claims made
concerning Dreiser as a naturalist, most of them hing-
ing upon the particular definition given the term
itself. "I would classify as naturalistic that type of
realism in which the individual is portrayed not merely
as subordinate to his background but as wholly de-

termined by it—that type of realism, in other words, in which the environment displaces its inhabitants in the role of the hero," Philip Rahv writes. "Theodore Dreiser, for example, comes as close as any American writer to plotting the careers of his characters strictly within a deterministic process."[14] *Sister Carrie* nearly fits this definition, but as we have seen, Dreiser provides moments, such as when Hurstwood is hesitating in front of the safe with the cash drawers in his hands, that can be interpreted both inside and outside the concept of determinism.

Another interpretation of naturalism is Stuart P. Sherman's: "A naturalistic novel is a presentation based upon a theory of animal behavior."[15] Dreiser certainly demonstrates that his characters are often *like* animals, but his major characters are always extended to the point where their actions (again Hurstwood in front of the safe provides the example) cannot be explained simply through instinct, breeding, or conditioning.

A more sophisticated view of naturalism, more sophisticated at least in understanding Dreiser, is provided in Donald Pizer's authoritative essay on the term in reference to nineteenth-century America. "The naturalist often describes his characters as though they are conditioned and controlled by environment, heredity, instinct, or chance," Pizer writes. "But he also suggests a compensating humanistic value in his characters or their fates which affirms the significance of the individual and of his life."[16] This affirmation is not so evident in *Sister Carrie* as it is in *Jennie Gerhardt,* but the fact remains that we are interested in Hurstwood not so much because of what Dreiser tells us about the coercive forces that act upon the saloon manager, but because of the value Dreiser assigns to Hurstwood's anguish.

The rise of naturalism in the American novel is often assigned to the dual influences of Darwinism (as preached by such writers as Thomas Henry Huxley and Herbert Spencer) and the example of French novelists such as Balzac and Zola—particularly the latter. These influences have been noted in Dreiser, who is known to have been acquainted with the work of these writers, and some commentators have argued that his reading of them had a direct and overwhelming impact on him. It is claimed that "Dreiser's art is inseparable from his view of reality; and that while Dreiser was composing *Sister Carrie* he was markedly influenced by the 'laws' of nature which Herbert Spencer described in his *First Principles*."[17] But there seems little need for Dreiser to have derived his naturalism from Spencer or any other outside source; as was suggested earlier, the ingredients for the doctrine Dreiser later reiterated were present in his early life. "The works of Dreiser's early phase," emphasizes one scholar, "are not . . . in a true sense, naturalistic in their views of life. While his first novel is colored by the terms of the so-called Darwinian or Spencerian philosophy, these terms do not shape the essential voice Dreiser the artist is trying to convey. This voice is rather the product of Dreiser's own experience. . ."[18] This is a point that Robert Penn Warren echoes in his *Homage to Theodore Dreiser*: "We must not assume . . . that in any simple sense, Dreiser took his ideas from Machiavelli, Spencer, Huxley and Darwin. Reading them merely gave form to ideas that Dreiser had, year after year, been living into."[19]

The literary influences on Dreiser are no more

easy to defend than the scientific ones. On this score
Dreiser is much harder to understand than his naturalistic predecessors in America: Frank Norris and Stephen
Crane. In the case of Norris, the French influence is
direct. Novels such as *McTeague* (1899) and *The
Octopus* (1901) clearly follow the theory of naturalism
put forth in Zola's *Le roman expérimental*: the idea
that the author sets up laboratory conditions in the
novel to test certain hypotheses about the conditions
of existence. These ideas are echoed in Norris's *The
Responsibilities of the Novelist* (1903). But the literary example provided Dreiser by Zola was hardly as
conscious a process in Dreiser's case. His mode of com-
position was not cold and slow; it was instead a violent
process fueled by his own experience.[20] Although
Dreiser did read Balzac and Zola and did know about
Crane and Norris, "no matter how [the] American
predecessors of Dreiser mirrored French realism in their
own works, these writers' influence on Dreiser will not
justify the assertion that Dreiser was really influenced
by French realism."[21] As Dreiser himself testified,
"personal observation and deduction were far more
valuable to me than any book."[22]

However indirect the scientific and literary influences were on Dreiser's thought, in his autobiographical
writings and often in the philosophical passages that
dot his novels he talks tough enough to shame even
Spencer. But Dreiser at his gloomiest is at worst an
inconsistent mechanist and often a reluctant naturalist
actually practicing a kind of humanism; "fortunately
for his greatness as a novelist, his explicit intellectual
vision of the world is not point for point congruous
with his vision as a novelist."[23]

But it is more accurate to see Dreiser against the
background of American naturalism and the conse-

quent mood of the 1890s than it is to talk about
specific influences. The way of thinking that has come
to be called naturalism and its attendant aesthetic
movements is, in a major sense, a result not so much
of Zola as of the pietistic movement in religion which
had been transferred to America by descendants of
Anabaptists, Quakers, and Moravians, "men who
preached a love of Being in general, of humanity for
its own sake rather than for specious moral virtues.
Ideal Christian love was a love for the unlovely, and
according to the pietistic psychology, the poor and the
socially immoral were not necessarily the worst sinners.
If ordinary love and virtue were the results of natural
law, then true virtue consisted only in the acceptance
of the universe as a whole."[24] Such ideas were preached
by the rebel Quaker Elias Hicks, who influenced Walt
Whitman's acceptance of life as a great spectacle and
the extension of the pietistic love of Being to sexual
love. Whitman's example was there for the naturalistic
painters and writers of the turn-of-the-century era. John
Sloan's paintings of New York are evidence of this in
his depiction of the city as a place of wonder yet a place
of implacable force and power, docks, warehouses,
elevated trains, and people both suffering and happy.
Dreiser is like Sloan; that is, "while his philosophical
speculations were often vague, his work exemplified the
stages in mood which begin in awe and wonder and
ended in the compassionate acceptance of the forces
of nature."[25]

　　And it is Dreiser's compassion that dominates in
his novels, not the naturalistic elements so widely emphasized in accounting for his importance. There is,
to be certain the power of environment and the influence of body chemistry present in all of his fiction,
but his significance cannot be explained by that: "His

greatness is in his insight, his sympathy, and his tragic
view of life."[26] Ultimately it does not seem to matter
so much that the careers of Carrie and Hurstwood are
fated. What seems more important is that in Carrie
we see the impossibility of realizing one's hopes. From
the start of the novel she is "dreaming wild dreams of
some vague, far-off supremacy. . ."[27] And at the end
she has that supremacy, her name in lights, her future
assured. But there she sits in a rocking chair, having
learned that she is still without happiness. The chair
is one of Dreiser's powerful, almost unconscious symbols. We first see Carrie boarding a train; we last see
her in a chair, rocking back and forth. She has trav-
eled far, but the train has turned into a rocking chair,
which will take her nowhere.

In Hurstwood we see an illustration of the opposite process: "The horror of a life in which all dreams
have been abandoned."[28] Hurstwood, like Carrie, has
his dreams; but unlike hers, his are not even realized
superficially. And at the end of Hurstwood's story,
Dreiser's subliminal symbolism enters again. Hurstwood
seals the crack at the bottom of his hotel-room door
with his coat and in reading about the act we are
invited to think back to that moment when Hurstwood
inadvertently (if indeed it was inadvertent) closed the
door of the safe. Such contrasting symbolism, such
sympathetic character portrayal, and such insight make
Dreiser's deterministic philosophy, as overexaggerated
as it usually is by his detractors, seem strangely beside
the point.

Even though Doubleday did little to promote the
book upon its first publication, its rejection was not as
complete as many have believed, nor was Dreiser subject to as much vilification as he sometimes later

claimed to have been. Actually *Sister Carrie* received a surprising number of favorable reviews. The Louisville *Times*, for example, drew a positive comparison between Dreiser and Norris, credited Dreiser with accurately depicting the grim side of life, and pronounced *Sister Carrie* "a remarkable book, strong, virile, written with the clear determination of a man who has a story to tell and who tells it."[29] The problem with the novel's first American publication was not so much that some reviews were not favorable, but simply that few periodicals bothered to comment on it. *The North American Review, Atlantic Monthly, Critic, Ainslee's Magazine*, the *Literary Digest*, the *Review of Reviews, The Dial, Outlook, The Nation*, and *Current Literature* all failed to review the book.[30] Despite Norris's personal efforts to promote the novel, undoubtedly the fact that Dreiser was virtually unknown as a writer contributed to the lack of attention the novel received.

But when *Sister Carrie* was reissued in 1907 it was given the attention that made it one of the most celebrated and heralded novels in literary history. It is widely assumed that changing attitudes in America, especially the anti-Victorian reaction that came in as the nineteenth century died, account for the success of *Sister Carrie* on the second time around. A more likely explanation derives from the 1901 publication of the novel in England, where the book appeared in Heinemann's Dollar Library series and immediately received many enthusiastic reviews. In commenting on the reaction of American critics when the novel was reissued here in 1907, Jack Salzman points out in his article on the "Fact and Fiction" of the publication of *Sister Carrie*, "that the most important reason for the changed response was the impression made on the American reviewers by the English critics."[31]

Present-day readers may find it difficult to understand what was so shocking and innovative about *Sister
Carrie* that the novel got the attention it did in 1907
(after all, there is no explicit sex in the book and no
four-letter vulgarisms), and it should be kept in mind
that the popular novels of the day included such books
as *Rebecca of Sunnybrook Farm* and *When Knight-
hood Was in Flower*. Dreiser was thought outrageous
not because of his language, not even because of his
subject matter, but because he presented Carrie without moral bias. Because he shows that her rise is a
result of her fall, he turns Victorian melodrama upside
down and creates what has been termed "the first truly
modern heroine in American fiction."[32] As a result of
this accomplishment, most subsequent American writers are in Dreiser's debt, as was acknowledged by
Sinclair Lewis when in his Nobel Prize acceptance
speech he said: "Dreiser's great first novel, *Sister Carrie*,
which he dared to publish thirty long years ago and
which I read twenty-five years ago, came to house-
bound and airless America like a great free Western
wind, and to our stuffy domesticity gave us the first
fresh air since Mark Twain and Whitman."[33] Unlikely
as it may have seemed, even to Dreiser himself in
1900, it is with *Sister Carrie* that the now dominant
liberal attitudes toward morality in the American novel
began.

Dreiser persisted in expressing those attitudes, although in a somewhat softer way, in *Jennie Gerhardt*,
his next novel, which appeared in 1911. To a certain
extent *Sister Carrie* is based on the experience of one
of Dreiser's sisters, who ran away to New York City
with a man who robbed his employers (Hannah and
Hogg's restaurant and bar in Chicago); *Jennie Gerhardt*

is drawn from the experience of another sister, who bore a child out of wedlock. But *Jennie Gerhardt* is much more autobiographical than Dreiser's first novel; in the Gerhardt family we get a picture of the Dreiser family that is little altered despite the use of Columbus, Ohio, as the initial setting. William Gerhardt, Jennie's father, is an unemployed religious fanatic (although a Lutheran and not, like Dreiser's father, a Catholic); the mother, in her gentleness and devotion to her children, is a reflection of Sarah Dreiser; and the Gerhardt household, as was the Dreiser household, is overpopulated. This return to his own past in seeking material for his fiction seems to have been a consequence of Dreiser's nervous breakdown; the writing of *Jennie Gerhardt* and *The "Genius"* (Dreiser's next and even more autobiographical novel) was a form of therapy, a means of reworking the conflicts and feelings of inadequacy stirred by memories of his youth.

The opening scene of poverty and despair that is basic to so many naturalistic novels is something that Dreiser did not have to imagine in terms of a scientific theory; he had lived it. *Jennie Gerhardt* begins in the fall of 1880 with Mrs. Gerhardt and Jennie, then 18, applying for scrubwork in Columbus's main hotel. They are desperate because Mr. Gerhardt is sick and winter is approaching. For weeks the family has been living on lye hominy, cornmeal mush, and fried potatoes. The regular charwoman had not shown up, so Mrs. Gerhardt is given a job scrubbing the marble stairs. Soon she receives permission to do the laundry for some of the hotel guests.

One day Jennie is asked to deliver a bundle of laundered clothing to Senator Brander, 52-years old and depressed by the loneliness in his life. Jennie is not beautiful, but the Senator is struck by the pathos surrounding her as well as by her sweet innocence. Jennie is the opposite of Carrie, much less self-centered and much more vulnerable. And Dreiser underscores this difference again and again, even though both characters very early become "fallen" women. "If Carrie is a weed equipped to thrust its way sunward against the hostility of its environment," Philip L. Gerber comments, "Jennie is the fragile blossom that, deprived of care and protection, will be trampled underfoot."[34] Senator Brander senses this quality in Jennie and he enters into an affair with her out of a spirit of protection as much as out of sexual impulse. Just as in *Sister Carrie,* what society puritanically deems a step down looks as if it will be a step up for Jennie. The Senator even has some idea of marrying her.

But then circumstance deals Jennie a blow: Senator Brander dies unexpectedly and Jennie is left, having just discovered that she is pregnant, to face the outrage of her moralistic father. After the baby Wilhelmina Vesta is born, Jennie joins her brother Bass in Cleveland, where he is working in a cigar store and she finds a place as a maid in the Bracebridge mansion. There she meets the second man in her life, Lester Kane, a house guest and wealthy bachelor of thirty-six.

Dreiser's chemisms begin to do their work and Lester is drawn to Jennie. He gives her gifts of money, takes her on a trip to New York, and eventually he establishes her in an apartment on Chicago's North Side. Their life is pleasant until Lester's family finds out about it and begins to pressure him to marry within his class. But Lester is reluctant to leave Jennie because she loves him so completely and unselfishly; and he has come to look upon Vesta as his own child.

A death, this time that of Lester's father, once again complicates matters for Jennie. Archibald Kane has ruled in his will that Lester must leave Jennie or make her his wife. If he leaves her, he will get the share of the estate that is rightfully his. If he marries her, he will receive only $10,000 a year for life, an amount considerably under what he is accustomed to. He is now 46 and not the passionate man he once was. Reluctantly, with considerable awareness of the unfairness involved, he gives in to his dead father's demands by leaving Jennie and marrying a woman of his own class.

Jennie is the victim, but her essential goodness keeps her from being victimized. She picks up as best she can and lives on despite the death of Vesta from typhoid fever. And later, when Lester is dying, he calls her to him and testifies that he has wanted only her, that she was the only woman he ever loved. "Jennie caught her breath," Dreiser writes. "It was the one thing she had waited for all these years—this testimony. It was the only thing that could make everything right —this confession of spiritual if not material union. Now she could live happily. Now die so."[35]

Jenny is left comfortably provided for by Lester, and she channels her capacity for love into raising two orphan children. But she is not quite as happy as her brave thoughts beside Lester's deathbed would have us believe. The novel ends as *Sister Carrie* begins—in a train station. But Jennie, instead of setting out on a journey, has just watched Lester's coffin being lifted into a baggage car. He is taken away in death and she is left with life. But what kind of life awaits her? "Before her was stretching a vista of lonely years down which she was steadily gazing," and she must ask, "Now what? She was not so old yet. There were those two orphan children to raise. They would marry and leave after a while, and then what? Days and days in endless

reiteration, and then—?"³⁶ Jennie is a heroine who elicits
our pity and respect, but her place in Dreiser's philosophy is much less obvious than the contrasting figure
of Carrie. Carrie is better equipped for survival; she
asks herself what she can get out of a situation. Jennie
is more sensitive, more internal; and she asks the more
profound question of why things have happened to
her the way they have.³⁷

In one sense, then, *Jennie Gerhardt*, is an advance
over *Sister Carrie*. But as a story it is simply less interesting, verging too closely upon a kind of sentimentality that threatens to turn the novel into a tear-jerker.
Dreiser, incidentally, originally came close to ruining
the novel by planning an ending in which Lester and
Jennie are married. Such a conclusion would have
defused the pathos out of which Jennie is created and
would have placed the novel outside Dreiser's conception of fate. As it is, the unperceptive reader is easily
enough led into a moralistic interpretation of the novel,
since Jennie does seem to pay for her sins. However,
the point Dreiser is making is, of course, anything but
that; he shows instead "that Jennie, in her unwavering
love for Lester Kane, proved that an illicit attachment
could embody more loyalty and goodness than a
church-sanctified marriage."³⁸

Given the reputation earned him by *Sister Carrie*,
Dreiser generally fared well at the hands of the critics
when *Jennie Gerhardt* appeared; however, he was again
attacked for his implied sexuality and his coarse style.
Some of the reviewers even went too far in their praise
of the novel, H. L. Mencken, for example, ranked
Jennie second in the history of American literature
only to *Huckleberry Finn*. The sale of the novel was
not good, however; while in the midst of a European
tour, to his great disappointment, Dreiser learned that

by the end of 1911 less than 8,000 copies had been sold. (It must be remembered that the sales of *Sister Carrie*, despite multiple reissuance, were not large—4,617 copies by September 1907 and another 5,248 copies by the end of 1908 in the cheap edition contracted by Grosset & Dunlap.[39] However, it continued to sell steadily for several years.)

But even though *Jennie Gerhardt* is far from being Dreiser's best novel, it should be given a unique place in the Dreiser canon. "*Jennie Gerhardt* is, in one sense, the most personal of Dreiser's novels," emphasizes Warren. "Here the man who was obsessed with sexuality, haunted by the fear of impotence, and unable to regard a woman as other than an anatomical convenience or to respect one as a person, the man who, by his own admission, was incapable of love, set out to write a novel about the definition of love."[40] And he achieves this definition through the sympathetic presentation of Jennie's personality, a presentation influenced by Dreiser's memories of his mother and perhaps stimulated by his unconscious search for a woman who would love him (and place as few demands upon him) as Jennie did Lester.

While it can be argued that in his attitude toward women Dreiser never reached maturity, he nonetheless remains one of the American writers most devoted to the study of feminine psychology. This can be seen in *A Gallery of Women*, one of his strangest, most unread, and in some ways underrated books.

Published in two volumes in 1929, although planned a decade earlier, *A Gallery of Women* is made up of sketches dealing with the women in his life. These sketches, many in the form of short stories, some almost short novels, are so frankly drawn from

actual events that Dreiser was accused of entering into
affairs simply to get material for his writing. Dreiser,
of course, intended the sketches to be shocking. When
he was outlining the project in 1919, he commented
in a letter to Mencken: "God, what a work! if I could
do it truly, ghosts of Puritans would rise and gibber in
the streets."[41] But when *A Gallery of Women* appeared it elicited little response from either the critics
or the public; however, it was the cause of some em-
barassment to those who recognized the portraits.

While the sections of *A Gallery of Women* that
deal with Dreiser's entanglements are of some biographical value, the major importance of the book is
that it shows the extent to which Dreiser was a student
of female behavior. One of the criticisms often leveled
at American literature is that so few American writers
are able to understand women. However, this is not
true of Dreiser. He was acquainted with many women,
and tried, as *A Gallery of Women* reveals, to tell their
stories with sympathy and understanding. The story
of Regina and her morphine addiction, the story of
Ernita and her conversion to communism, the story of
Giff the fortune teller, and the stories of many others
are all retold with compassion. In some, such as the
stories of Ernita and Giff, there is no sexual involvement between Dreiser and the woman whose experiences he is recounting, and as a whole the sympathetic
sketches render invalid the notion that Dreiser regarded women as mere objects.

What these sketches explain again and again is
how Dreiser could write books like *Sister Carrie* and
Jennie Gerhardt. As aloof, as brusque, as self-pitying
as he was, he had a degree of curiosity for which he is
generally not given credit. This curiosity was repeatedly
directed at discovering the particular fate those with

whom he came in contact contained within themselves. And when he discovered it, he wrote with a sense of amazement that individual life goes on the way it does. As Matthiessen emphasizes, Dreiser "has very little of the psychologist's skill in portraying the inner life of his characters, but he is caught by an overwhelming sense of the flow of life, mysterious beyond any probing."[42] In his subsequent books, Dreiser turned to the mysteries of the artistic consciousness, the business mind, the vagaries of guilt and innocence, and the growth of religious belief. But the kind of wonder he expresses in his studies of women is perhaps one of his most engaging qualities, a quality that is rare in American writing—and Dreiser would not be unflattered to be remembered as a ladies' man, especially in this sense.

3

Dreiser's

Men

It has been one of my commonest experiences, and one of the most interesting to me, to note that nearly all of my keenest experiences intellectually, my most gorgeous *rapprochements* and swiftest developments mentally, have been by, to, and through men, not women, although there have been several exceptions to this.

—*Twelve Men*

Just as few events occur abruptly in Dreiser's novels, so his career cannot be understood in terms of sudden and dramatic changes. But after *Jennie Gerhardt*, a shift takes place in Dreiser's writing that is not easily explainable. In his first two novels, Dreiser writes about his family and himself only indirectly, choosing women as his central characters, and developing his stories with some measure of control, if not absolute economy. But in his subsequent novels, Dreiser puts more of himself into his books, choosing men as his central characters and writing much more prolixly. This turn toward deeper personal involvement, while it undoubtedly contributed to the structural weaknesses in *The "Genius,"* A *Trilogy of Desire*, *The Bulwark*, and even in his generally acknowledged masterpiece, *An American Tragedy*, brought out a side of Dreiser that is not so apparent in his early work—his sentimentality. This trait is, of course, a factor in the duality basic to Dreiser's life and accomplishment; he was a sentimentalist despite the moral detachment he strove to affect. His essential setting, the post-industrial revolution, the post-Darwinian American jungle remains more or less unchanged after *Jennie Gerhardt*; but Dreiser's reactions to the feelings of his protagonists undergo a change in the direction of increased sympathy.

This change can best be seen in *The "Genius,"* a frankly autobiographical novel that foreshadows in many ways (its 736–page length not the least of them) Thomas Wolfe's *Look Homeward, Angel*. In *The "Genius,"* Dreiser tells his own story up through the loss of his job at Butterick's. But the novel is much more than a veiled retelling of Dreiser's experiences; it is also an evaluation of the role of the artist in American culture. And *The "Genius"* is one other thing as well; like all of Dreiser's novels, it gives us a graphic account of an era.

Once again Dreiser returns to the midwest to begin his narrative, this time to Alexandria, Illinois. Eugene Witla is the mooncalf son of a sewing machine and insurance salesman. At first Eugene has no particularly overwhelming ambitions, outside of a raging interest in girls. He grows up, has an adolescent romance, and eventually, because he seems unsuited for anything else, he is given a job as an apprentice typesetter in the local newspaper office. Then one Sunday afternoon as he is lying in a hammock, the inevitable Dreiserian thought hits him—he will go to Chicago. He tells his parents that he intends to catch the four o'clock train that day, and he does.

"The city of Chicago—who shall portray it!"[1] With these words Dreiser introduces Eugene to the city and also links himself to his hero. Eugene, like Dreiser, is to become the portrayer of cities, the practitioner of a bold, revolutionary form of art in which the ugly forces of the industrial state serve to inspire visions of a paradoxically grim beauty. Eugene goes through a series of jobs (stove polisher, laundry driver, bill collector) before he moves toward his destiny by taking lessons at the Art Institute. There he first realizes the extent of his talent and starts taking himself seriously as an artist. He is gradually drawn into the underground world of painters and models, and soon he has an affair with one of the girls. In addition, his lessons lead to a job as an illustrator for a newspaper and to thoughts about trying his luck in New York City.

While amid his struggles in Chicago, Eugene briefly returns home to Alexandria, and there he encounters a woman whose presence haunts him throughout the rest of the book. She is Angela Blue, a visiting schoolteacher from Blackwood, Wisconsin. Eugene eventually proposes to her, goes to New York and establishes a reputation as a painter, falls out of love with her during that interim, but marries her anyway. The rest of Eugene's story deals with his disillusionment over married life and his problems as an artist.

Once in New York, he slowly catches on as a magazine illustrator, then secures a show for himself in a prestigious private gallery. His painting of street scenes, tug boats on the Hudson, railroad yards, and other aspects of city life create a sensation. He and Angela are able to afford a tour of Europe and things seem set. But then Eugene's nerves start to fail him. Like Dreiser himself, Eugene suffers a nervous breakdown, regaining his health only after a time of manual labor in a railroad carpentry shop and mill.

When Eugene returns to the city it is to work in the new and growing advertising industry as an artist and then as a director. For the first time in his life he is making a large and steady income. He climbs the corporate ladder, eventually becoming managing director of a publishing firm at $25,000 a year. But his marital dissatisfactions and the crisis of impending middle age catch up with him. He falls in love with Suzanne Dale, a beautiful debutante, and plans to run off with her; however, her mother finds out, informs Eugene's boss, and Eugene is asked to leave the company. To complicate matters, Angela has finally, after many years of longing for a baby, succeeded in getting pregnant. Suzanne is taken to Europe by her mother, Eugene separates from Angela, and the second downward spiral in the novel spins faster and faster. Eugene goes to live in a single room, walks the streets, and tries to pull himself together through reading odd philosophic and religious volumes. An interesting part of Eugene's attempt at rehabilitation is that he seeks help through Christian Science, which was then a controversial and increasingly popular religious movement.

Eugene's story, in contrast to those of Carrie and Jennie, takes a turn upward at the end, even though he has lost Suzanne and Angela dies after childbirth. The novel concludes with Eugene, having once again become a successful painter, living in suburban comfort and raising his daughter. He walks out onto his lawn in the late November night and wonders: "Where in all this—in substance, is Angela? Where in substance will be that which is me? What a sweet welter life is —how rich, how tender, how grim, how like a colorful symphony."[2]

This note of speculation underscores one of Dreiser's lifelong characteristics as a writer. Contrary to the impression gained by reading only one of Dreiser's novels, such as *Sister Carrie,* he is not an advocate of programs and philosophies. In most of his books he is more the searcher than the finder, more the questioner than the answerer. Even when Eugene finds that Christian Science helps him, Dreiser does not endorse it. To Dreiser, as to Eugene, life is seen as a symphony made up of many movements, produced by disparate forces, and traceable only to the mind of the composer, which is in itself a mystery.

Throughout the novel Eugene asks questions as he tries to move toward an understanding of himself and his world. "What is life anyway?" he asks. "What is the human body? What produces passion? Here we are for a few years surging with a fever of longing and then we burn out and die."[3] Can life be explained through chemistry? "Tendencies are subtle things," Dreiser writes. "They are involved in the chemistry of one's being, and those who delve in the mysteries of biology frequently find that curious anomaly, a form of minute animal life born to be the prey of another form of animal life—chemically and physically attracted to its own disaster."[4] Will this explain why some people fail and others succeed? Or is it to be understood in terms of big fish eating little fish? The question haunts Eugene as it was to continue to haunt Dreiser.

Eugene's speculations undergo modification one day when he goes to a morgue. There he "saw human bodies apparently dissolving into a kind of chemical mush, and he had said to himself then how ridiculous it was to assume that life meant anything much to the forces which were doing these things. Great chemical and physical forces were at work, which permitted, accidentally perhaps, some little shadow-play, which would soon pass. But, oh, its presence—how sweet it was!"[5] Dreiser's peculiar sentimentality, his reaction to the gruesome realities of biology and physics with which he repeatedly wrestles in his novels, is brought out by this passage. Life may be all chemistry and decay, but it is also a shadow-show from which we get our reasons for living and through which our art is justified.

The "Genius" itself is a shadow-show, Dreiser's attempt to capture images of himself. As Dreiser once said of the novel, "Some people think I like *Sister Carrie* the best. I like *The 'Genius'* best of all. There's more of myself in it."[6] His own fascination with the city, his obsession with women, his mental problems, his rise and fall as an editor, and his own decision to survive as an artist are all portrayed in Eugene, in painful detail. The section of the novel in which the breakup of Eugene's marriage is described must be considered one of the most agonizingly personal passages Dreiser ever wrote.

But though the piling up of detail in *The "Genius"* is a virtue in the most crucial moments of the story, it is unfortunately cumbersome in many other places. The plot Dreiser was working his way through is obviously so close to his own experience that omission of incidents and conversations less than incidental to the book's development was apparently impossible for him, a point on which several critics have commented.[7] What resulted is dialogue whose sole *raison d'être* is that Dreiser could not get it out of his head any other way; even the most conscientious reader is inclined to begin skimming.

Floyd Dell, who was responsible for editing the novel, apparently tried to do some cutting (in spite of Dreiser's objections), but just how much trimming was done is uncertain. Excess baggage is a fault that is not so evident in *Sister Carrie* and *Jennie Gerhardt*, but is increasingly evident in Dreiser's later novels. However, the denouement of *The "Genius"* in Angela's death is made all the more effective by the hundreds of pages that precede it. On many of these pages Eugene is shown wishing that he were released from Angela; but when she does die, he is shocked at the suddenness of it. At the end of all the words Dreiser has used to describe Eugene's frustrations, he offers us two taut and strikingly effective sentences: "So he had his wish. She was really dead."[8] These sentences do much to justify the tedium which has preceded them.

Even though *The "Genius"* is over-long, there is a ring of authority to it, and this too somewhat excuses its length. Eugene's rise in the advertising and publishing business is depicted in a believable way simply because Dreiser knew what he was writing about; he had made the same ascent. Other memorable sections of the novel—the delivery room where Angela has her baby, for instance—are the product of Dreiser's research (curiosity might be a better word). But throughout, there is the same sense of reality that is found in Dreiser's earlier writing and also in the "Ashcan" school of verist painters with which Eugene is identified. (Dreiser took some of the details used in Eugene's experience as a painter from the life of Everett Shinn, one of Dreiser's friends and also a practitioner of the new realism in painting.) That Dreiser made Eugene a painter shows, by the way, the relationship Dreiser perceived between what he was doing in writing and what the new wave of American artists was doing on canvas.

Strangely enough, Dreiser's realism is lacking in the one area that made the novel seem so infamous when it appeared—the portrayal of sexual and romantic relationships. Dreiser's lovers almost always employ the bizarre language of the Victorian romance. Here is how Dreiser handles one encounter between Eugene and Suzanne: "Let's choose new names for each, so that we'll know who's calling," Eugene says. "You shall be Jenny Lind and I Allan Poe." Dreiser concludes this dreamy interlude by writing, "Then they fell to ardent love-making until the time came when they had to return."[9] The defect here is partly due to Dreiser's place in time. He is one of the first American writers to attempt to deal honestly with sexuality, but his problem is that he lacked a suitable vocabulary. It is a lack that Dreiser shares with his contemporaries; Norris, London, Lewis, and even Sherwood Anderson (who tried more openly than the rest to deal with sexual themes) all lapse into a general kind of silliness when trying to depict men and women in love. This silliness is often a surprise to readers because of the reputation of these writers as realists. Their realism is, of course, social, not sexual.

This is because in describing sexual relationships, aside from pornography, there was no model to follow other than the indirectness, for example, of writers such as George Eliot and Thomas Hardy in England, or the often coy brutality of Zola and Balzac in France. A way had to be found of representing actions that formerly had been avoided in most "serious" literature. With no useful tradition behind him, Dreiser had to do the best he could for Eugene and Suzanne. While what he did was not good enough, it was at least a beginning that later writers were to improve upon. However, in Fitzgerald, Hemingway, Steinbeck, and surprisingly enough in D. H. Lawrence, one still often finds an awkwardness, a clumsy kind of uncertainty, in developing sexual scenes. Passionate moments in novels remain elusive even now.

Another reason for the failure of Dreiser's love scenes can be traced to his sentimentality. Though, as we have seen, he had relationships with many women and used some of them cruelly, in writing about them, he seemed to be unable to repress an essential tenderness that at times is expressed in as syrupy a manner as the worst of his brother Paul's songs. But then, as Warren maintains, "Theodore Dreiser and Paul Dresser were cut off the same bolt of goods—the only difference being that one was a genius."[10] Another of the ironies concerning Dreiser is that the mood and often the language in some of the scenes that got *The "Genius"* banned unconsciously echoed the sheet-music lyrics of the day. "One kiss, sweet, in parting," breathes Eugene to Suzanne. "One. Life has opened anew for me."[11]

Although completed before *The Financier* and

The Titan, The "Genius" was not published until John
Lane and Co. brought it out in September 1915. The
reviews were quite negative, as might be expected given
the importance of Eugene's love life in the book. But
some of the reaction was based on anti-German senti-
ment (the war in Europe had made it a liability for
an American writer to have a German name). A typical attitude toward *The "Genius"* is indicated in a
headline that appeared October 9 in the *Brooklyn
Eagle:* "A GENIUS AND ALSO A CUR." The novel
was attacked for, among other things, its sexual obsession, its length, and its paganism in such leading
magazines as *Harper's Weekly* and *The Nation.* Even
some of Dreiser's most loyal sympathizers, including
Edgar Lee Masters and Mencken had their doubts
about it.[12] Sales totaled an unimpressive 8,500 through
June 1916, although when reissued by Liveright in
1923 it sold 12,301 copies by the end of the year.

Opinions have remained generally unpositive ever
since. Matthiessen is representative of most commentators in maintaining that *The "Genius"* is Dreiser's
poorest novel, containing some of his worst writing.[13]
Warren is not any more charitable. "We may sur-
mise," he writes, "that the elements of self-indulgence
and self-vindication that appear so nakedly in *The
'Genius'* constitute one of the reasons, perhaps the
basic reason, for the book's being the crashing bore
that it is."[14] Some critics, such as the poet John Berryman, while not exactly apologizing for the novel, have
testified that it has an odd kind of appeal, perhaps
because of its personal nature (Berryman admitted to
having read it, "four or five times just for pleasure"[15]).
And at least one, Walter Blackstock, is willing to
defend it for its theme, the "achievement of responsible selfhood as an artist."[16]

While *The "Genius"* is far from being a well
written or even very readable novel, it is equally far
from being unimportant. As flawed as it is, it is nonetheless a valuable account of Dreiser's own struggles
as an artist as well as an expression of his own uncertainty over his talent (the quotation marks in the
title indicate this). And it also occupies its own significant place in the history of American literature,
something that is now too often overlooked. "The
chief thing we have to remind ourselves of in connec-
tion with *The 'Genius'* is why it is an important book,"
Matthiessen writes regarding the date of the novel's
publication. "The situation in American literature was
still substantially the same as it had been when Henry
Adams noted that except for Whitman no American
artist 'had ever insisted on the power of sex, as every
classic had always done.' "[17] As bad as it may be, *The
"Genius,"* at least as a publishing event, has to be
regarded as one of the most prominent American
novels, if one of the deservedly most unread.

If *The "Genius"* is personal to the point of giving
us Dreiser's self-conception, the *Trilogy of Desire* is
personal in another sense—giving us Dreiser as he
would have liked to be. In the *Trilogy* we have the
rise and fall of an American type Dreiser greatly ad-
mired and envied, although because of his Progressive
background could never endorse—the financial wizard,
the robber baron personified in the hero of the *Trilogy*,
Frank Algernon Cowperwood. For his portrait of Cowperwood, Dreiser went to the life of an infamous late
nineteenth-century Chicago streetcar tycoon, Charles
Tyson Yerkes, often doing little more to fictionalize
the events in Yerkes's life than to change names. The
result is a new type of novel for Dreiser, based almost

totally on research (for his facts Dreiser pored through newspaper files and went to Chicago, Philadelphia, and Europe to retrace Yerkes's career) and drawing only incidentally from Dreiser's past (some of Cowperwood's amatory involvements are based on Dreiser's own). But despite the departure in technique, the *Trilogy* manifests many of the same weaknesses that appeared in *The "Genius"*—including its unjustifiable length and unrealistic dialogue (especially in the love scenes).

The Financier (1912), the first volume of the *Trilogy* begins a narrative that is essentially a retelling of the standard Horatio Alger rags-to-riches story, a myth that Dreiser philosophizes over considerably. "In *Sister Carrie* he had, indeed, treated the myth, draining it of its moral content by setting it against the mechanics of success and failure," Warren writes; "but now he undertook to anatomize it more fully with all his deep ambivalences in its psychological, social, moral, and metaphysical aspects. It hardly seems an accident that the name 'Alger' is absorbed into the name of his hero—Frank Algernon Cowperwood."[18] Frank, the son of a banker in pre-Civil War Philadelphia, does not actually begin in poverty, but his life nonetheless represents an incredible upward progression. When his Uncle Seneca asks him what he is most interested in, Frank tells him that it is one thing—money. Frank, of course, later develops an obsessive interest in women, and Dreiser's *Trilogy* literally becomes one of desire— Frank's desire for wealth and sex.

The code that guides Frank is early symbolized in what is the most famous scene in the entire *Trilogy*. At the age of ten Frank asks the crucial question: How is life organized? He receives his answer in a fish tank at a market not far from his home. A squid and a lobster occupy the tank. The squid is the lobster's prey, and piece-by-piece the helpless invertebrate disappears. This little drama provides Frank with his answer: "Things lived on each other—that was it. Lobsters lived on squids and other things. What lived on lobsters? Men, of course! Sure that was it! And what lived on men? he asked himself. . . . Sure, men lived on men."[19] From this meditation Frank derives his system of ethics.

Another early episode shows Frank how he can go about living on other men. His curiosity draws him into a wholesale grocery auction just in time to hear the auctioneer trying to sell seven cases of Castile soap, the same kind of soap Frank's family grocer sells. Frank bids on the soap, gets it for thirty-two dollars. He then persuades the grocer to pay sixty-two dollars for it, borrows thirty-two dollars from Mr. Cowperwood to cover the original bid, and pockets his first financial killing.

A few years later he works himself into the brokerage business, and the sharpness he precociously demonstrated is transformed into the aggressive wheeling and dealing that makes him a millionaire in his twenties. He has also, by that time, married a beautiful widow, Lillian Semple, five years his senior. The Civil War begins and Frank, thanks to his financial genius, turns national disaster into private profit. But then the first of his woman problems develops when he falls in love with Aileen Butler, daughter of one of the most powerful contractors in Philadelphia. Old Mr. Butler learns about the liaison. When the Chicago fire initiates a panic in the stock market and Frank is caught with his resources overextended, Butler is instrumental in getting Frank convicted of larceny (one of Frank's deals involved transferring $60,000 from the

treasury of the city of Philadelphia into his own account). Frank's appeal is denied and he goes to prison.

He emerges in 1873 just in time to take advantage
of the panic brought about when Jay Cooke & Co.,
then the foremost financial organization in the United
States, closed its doors. During a single weekend Frank
becomes a millionaire again. He decides to take his
fortune and go to Chicago for a fresh start. At this
point, after some Dreiserian speculation that Frank is
like both the black grouper (an exceedingly deceptive
fish, possessing the ability to change color) and Macbeth (because the Weird Sisters of Fate always seem
to have something ominous to say about the man who
is dominated by ambition), *The Financier* ends.

Although most of *The Financier* was not finished
until some time after *The "Genius,"* Harper's encouraged Dreiser to follow *Jennie Gerhardt* with the first
installment of the Cowperwood saga. Officials in the
publishing house were afraid that *The "Genius,"* again
because of its sexuality, would get them into trouble
(perhaps if they had known what was coming in *The
Titan*, they would not have been so eager to suggest
that Dreiser concentrate on getting *The Financier* into
publishable condition). For the moment, however, they
had made a wise decision; *The Financier* was well received, many reviewers praising it for its detail, and
sales totaled 8,322 in the last three months of 1912
(although they dropped off in the next year).

In writing about the businessman-financier, Dreiser
seemed to be following in what was already a well-
established genre that included such previous novels
as H. H. Boyesen's *A Daughter of the Philistines*
(1883), William Dean Howells's *A Hazard of New
Fortunes* (1889), Norris's *The Pit* (1903), Robert

Herrick's *Memoirs of an American Citizen* (1905), David Graham Phillips's *The Master Rogue* (1905), and Upton Sinclair's *The Metropolis* (1907), and *The Moneychangers* (1908), as well as Edith Wharton's later *The Custom of the Country* (1913). But there is a great difference between these novels and Dreiser's *Trilogy*; instead of briefly summarizing his hero's deals, Dreiser recounts and explains them in incredible detail. This serves to embed Cowperwood in the actual financial world in a way that none of Dreiser's predecessors can match.

The documentation of Frank's financial life continues in *The Titan* (1914), but it must share space with a lesser but more scandalous kind of documentation, that of Frank's promiscuity. Because of the sex scenes in the book and also because of a suit threatened by Emilie Grigsby, one of Yerkes's mistresses, Harper's decided not to publish *The Titan* even though 8,500 sets of sheets had been printed. But the John Lane Co. of London was willing to take Dreiser on, and the novel finally appeared in May, 1914.

The Titan opens with Frank divorcing Lillian and marrying Aileen. His financial success continues with his involvement in the Chicago gas companies and the street railroads. He eventually gains control of the city streetcar system, renews his interest in collecting art, and he and Aileen begin to entertain in hope of social prominence. But their social life is blighted as soon as Frank starts to make enemies through his business practices. In addition, the news of his past catches up with him, and he and Aileen find themselves outcasts. Frank gradually tires of Aileen and his life soon becomes a succession of philanderings. The validity of the Macbeth-like prophecy with which *The Financier* ends, rapidly becomes apparent: "Hail to you, Frank Cowperwood, master and no master, prince of a world of dreams whose reality was disillusion!"[20]

Frank's troubles continue to pile up as the Macbeth analogy extends through the novel. Aileen is unfaithful to him—and lets him know about it. He has difficulty getting backing when he wants to get in on the development of elevated railroads. But his pride and innate confidence carry him through the crisis of Aileen's unfaithfulness; and his gift of a $300,000 telescope to the University of Chicago (something Yerkes actually did) just when his financial outlook is bleakest gains him the support and trust of the banking men. Before long Frank is worth $20 million. "And yet," Dreiser writes, "he was coming to feel that, no matter how complete his financial victory might ultimately be, the chances were that he and Aileen would never be socially accepted here in Chicago."[21] After making a killing in the panic of 1896, Frank therefore builds a mansion in New York, where he and Aileen might find acceptance.

The Chicago involvements continue, of course, with Frank at one point trying to bribe the governor of the state, in order to retain an advantageous franchise position. His philandering also continues, reaching a level where Aileen, thoroughly depressed by it all, attempts suicide. A disaster of another sort follows when the Chicago city council, despite Frank's ready offer of lucrative compensation, responds to public pressure and rejects an ordinance that would have given him a fifty-year transit franchise. The titan is brought down, but not yet destroyed. He turns to Berenice Fleming, his latest and most ideal love, and the second part of the *Trilogy* ends with Dreiser asking the by-now less-than-rhetorical question, "why did the weird sisters plan ruin to the murderous Scot?"[22]

The critical reception of *The Titan* was unenthusiastic. Ford Madox Ford maintained that he could not read beyond the eleventh seduction,[23] and though Mencken and James Gibbons Huneker praised the book, they were in the minority. Arthur Guiterman's rhymed review in the June 18, 1914, issue of *Life* set the tone for most of the commentary:

> Your hero's morals must be lax
> To make a novel realistic,
> But when the ladies come in packs
> Its getting much too Mormonistic.

The book sold poorly—only 8,016 copies by the end of the year—and Dreiser once again found himself with a smaller financial return than he had expected (another one of the many ironies in his life, given the ease with which Frank makes fortune after fortune).

For the conclusion of Frank's story, readers had to wait until 1947 when Doubleday published *The Stoic*. Although the final volume of the *Trilogy* did not appear until after Dreiser's death, he worked on it off-and-on throughout the 1920s and 1930s. Its completion was, of course, delayed by the poor reception given *The Titan* and by Dreiser's need to work on more financially rewarding projects. He was also held back by uncertainty over how to end the Cowperwood story, an uncertainty that is by no means resolved in the ending that Dreiser finally decided to tack on.

Frank is nearing sixty and his Chicago career is at an end as *The Stoic* begins. He could retire, but instead he turns his attention to England and the London transit industry. He also directs his attention toward Berenice, and to distract his jealous wife he hires a gigolo, Bruce Tollifer, to entertain her; but Aileen learns the truth and the marital split that Frank, largely to keep up appearances, has long tried to avert, becomes a dangerous possibility. What makes Frank's personal life all the more complicated is that in Berenice he thinks he has finally found his soulmate.

But before Frank can complete his London dealings and before his personal difficulties can be resolved, his health fails and he dies—that suddenly. He leaves an elaborate will that, among other things, provides for the establishment of a hospital in the Bronx. However, as Dreiser solemnly notes, "Cowperwood had failed to take into consideration . . . the workings of the American courts throughout the nation; the administration of justice or the lack of it; the length of time American lawyers were capable of delaying a settlement in any of these courts."[24] As a consequence, Frank's fortune dissolves within a few years after he is placed in his custom-designed, modified-Ionic tomb. His fate is the same as Macbeth's— all his ruthless ambition has gotten him is death.

Dreiser continued working on *The Stoic* until a day before he died (a fact that lends a certain poignancy to the death scene in the novel—Dreiser must have been thinking of his own death as he wrote it), but the book was slightly unfinished. Dreiser made his intention clear, however: Berenice was to become a nurse, devote herself to helping others, and work to raise the funds for the hospital Frank had hoped would be financed by his fortune.

Though Dreiser had intended the ending of *The Stoic* to be noble and moving, it does not quite work. The change Berenice undergoes (partly as a result of a trip to India where she learns to pity the suffering

multitudes and where she also studies under a guru)
is not very believable. As Elias emphasizes, Dreiser
"knew that the ending would go beyond his original
plan, beyond the reflection that all was vanity and
that wealth was, at the last, only the tombstone in the
cemetery. It would now bring forth a redeeming aspect,
something to excuse Cowperwood; it would emphasize
his search for beauty and enable Berenice, through
immersion in the lore of Yoga, to perceive the meaning in all that had occurred."[25] Yet the ending is
handled in such a way that it is not acceptable. Dreiser
tries to make us believe in Berenice's intellectual sen-
sitivity by having her display her devotion to Emily
Brontë's "Last Lines," which he reproduces in its en-
tirety, although the first stanza is bad enough:

> No coward soul is mine
> No trembler in the world's storm-troubled sphere
> I see Heaven's glories shine
> And Faith shines equal, arming me from fear.

The effect is the opposite of what he intended,
leaving one to conclude that Dreiser's lack of sophistication, perhaps a consequence of his haphazard self-
education, is nowhere more apparent than in the last
pages of *The Stoic*. The novel was, of course, pronounced inferior by most critics when it came out.

Despite the many defects in the *Trilogy of
Desire*, the scope of Dreiser's attempt provides partial
compensation. The work is certainly too sprawling,
too many characters cross the pages only to disappear
within a few sentences, and too often scenes that could
be easily summarized and passed over are given need-
less documentation. (In *The Financier*, Dreiser even
went so far as to produce lengthy transcripts from
Frank's trial.) Frank himself never seems to come to

life even though, as Matthiessen points out, "Dreiser envisaged as great heroic stature in Cowperwood as Marlowe did in Tamburlaine or Melville in Ahab. But Dreiser's method here was that of the historical novel, and he proceeded to involve his hero not only with the dominant forces of his time, but also with its detailed surfaces."[26]

Dreiser does provide a relatively complete and convincing account of Frank's financial manipulations and the trilogy could be read as a history of 19th-century American economic practices. While this aspect of the trilogy is its most memorable, it also contributes to the unreadableness of the work: "Unfortunately the body lacks a heart, remains inert. There is a failure not of documentation but of imagination."[27] Almost everyone is interested in money, but it is difficult for a writer to make the cold actualities of money-grubbing seem interesting, even when high finance is involved. Nonetheless, one is forced to respect the sheer energy Dreiser put into what is certainly among the most ambitious series of novels written in this century.

A further point should be made concerning Frank's fall and the evaporation of his fortune. The meaninglessness of his life might at first appear to be in contradiction with Dreiser's philosophy, at least as that philosophy has been popularly understood. While Spencerian and Nietzschean superman overtones sound throughout the *Trilogy*, Dreiser was, it must be remembered, influenced by Progressivism. Frank is a robber baron (the word "Titan" was synonomous with that term during the 1890s), a type constantly under fire during Dreiser's early writing career; and Frank's dismal end is strictly in accordance with the muckrakers' predictions. But, Dreiser's efforts to make

Frank's career be seen against the background of natural processes and the inscrutable vagaries of history
take him considerably beyond the frame of reference
found in most of the writing that comes out of the
Progressive era—so far beyond that Warren has termed
him a "cosmic Muckraker."[28]

Dreiser's cosmic interests take another turn in a
novel that is best understood when compared to the
story of Frank Cowperwood. *The Bulwark* is yet another variation on the Horatio Alger formula, but it
is a considerably different look at the turn of the
century business world. Although not published until
1946, *The Bulwark* has its roots in the same period in
his life that saw the generation of *The "Genius"* and
the *Trilogy*. Dreiser got the idea for it from a story
told him in 1912 by Anna Tatum, a young Wellesley
graduate who was one of his admirers (unlike more
discreet writers, Dreiser often encouraged visits from
the unknown women who had become interested in his
writing). The story concerned her father whose Quaker
beliefs, instead of leading to a life of quiet satisfaction
and harmony, brought his family tragedy. "The irony
of it was in perfect accord with Dreiser's conviction—
gleaned in part from his father's career—that religion,
however idealistic, failed to meet reality and indeed, in
its repression of 'natural' impulses, led to disaster,"
Swanberg writes.[29]

Dreiser began organizing *The Bulwark* at once,
little knowing that over three decades would pass before the novel would be finished and that his original
plan would change from a story showing the gap between religious idealism and the realities of life to a
story in which religion provides an answer to the
vagaries of twentieth-century existence.

The Bulwark at first seems to be an anomaly among Dreiser's other novels, and more than one critic has suggested that it is difficult to credit it to the author of the *Trilogy*.[30] While it takes the shape of the Dreiserian novel, (that is, it is a fictional biography), *The Bulwark* ends more softly, more positively than any of Dreiser's major books. It is one of the major problems in categorizing Dreiser as a naturalistic writer, but for the reader aware of Dreiser's sentimentality, his constant tendency toward the kind of metaphysical speculation that borders on mysticism, and his distaste for the way of the world, *The Bulwark* need not seem strange at all.

Solon Barnes, the hero of *The Bulwark* and the bulwark himself, is born into a Quaker family during the second half of the last century. His family background is crucial, for he remains a Quaker the rest of his life, during which he becomes a successful Philadelphia bank treasurer and fathers five children. His story develops around two conflicts, both involving his religion. As the new century begins and his children start to grow up, they find their father's religion to be out-of-date and too restrictive. They rebel in various ways: Isobel studies the new psychology, Orville becomes a conservative and money-hungry dullard, Dorothen a mindless denizen of high society, Etta the mistress of a New York artist (who is reminiscent of Eugene Witla), and Stewart a playboy. While his children are going their separate ways, Solon has increasing difficulty squaring his Quakerism with the current and less-than-honest banking procedures (procedures of the sort Frank Cowperwood turned to his own advantage).

The double pressure on Solon mounts until Stewart, who is his youngest child, commits suicide in jail after being involved in a sordid rape-murder. This, coupled with Solon's realization that the business with which he is connected was becoming increasingly corrupt, leads to his resignation from the bank. "He had been no less guilty than these others," Dreiser writes of Solon and his fellow bank officers, "sitting beside them as director and furthering their schemes for the lunatic accumulation of wealth: money that meant only such unnecessary luxuries and pleasures as had been flaunted before the eyes of Stewart and had finally destroyed him."[31] Solon retires only to face the death of his wife (whom he has steadfastly loved—certainly a rarity among Dreiser's characters) and the deterioration of his health. Yet, like Job, he remains a bulwark of his faith, finding comfort and strength through a deeper understanding of his beliefs, despite the despair that he must deal with daily. And he dies with this meditation on his lips: "If thee does not turn to the Inner Light, where will thee go?"[32]

Solon Barnes's last question is, of course, the central question in the book and makes the novel into more of a sermon than one ordinarily expects from Dreiser. The mystic belief in a universal force of creativity that is present in Quakerism and centralized in American Transcendentalism (which, as has been already emphasized, is basic to Dreiser's naturalism) is what carries Solon through. The turning away from this belief toward the pursuit of material pleasures or other forms of worldliness is what destroyed Stewart, corrupted the rest of Solon's children (although Etta finally profits by her father's example and turns back toward the old faith), and may crumble all of twentieth-century America. *The Bulwark* is not simply a study of the Quaker tradition in the United States; it is an endorsement of the type of life Solon Barnes represents, albeit a somewhat peculiar endorsement from the pen of a man who did not let the book interfere with his own libertinism.

But the central point in *The Bulwark* is not so surprising when one considers the endless abstruse questioning that goes on in the other novels, questioning that inevitably can find answers only in mysticism. Dreiser a Quaker? It is not farfetched at all, although he never did actually turn into a Solon Barnes. As fascinated as Dreiser was with the amorality of a Carrie and the Machiavellian operations of a Frank Cowperwood, there is always a faint suggestion of disapproval (especially in the *Trilogy*), as if the voice of Solon is present all along. And he tried to balance his characters out. For Carrie there is Jennie, and for Frank there is Solon, who derives from roughly the same era as Frank, is somewhat similarly involved in the world of finance, and is Frank as he ought to be, given the Quaker ethic. That Dreiser intended Solon to be Frank's counterpart is indicated in a scene at the end of *The Bulwark* that parallels the fish tank scene in *The Financier*:

One day, walking the paths around Lever Creek, Solon was arrested by the various vegetative and insect forms obviously devised and energized by the Creative Force that created all things in apparently endless variety of designs and colors. Here now on a long-stalked plant reaching up about four feet, and on the end of a small twig that bore a small bud, obviously a blossom of some type, was perched, and eating the bud, an exquisitely colored and designed green fly so green and translucent that it reminded one of an emerald, only it was of a much more tender and vivid texture. . . . Why was this beautiful creature, whose design so delighted him, compelled to feed upon another living creature, a beautiful flower? For obviously, as it ate, it was destroying the bud of this plant. . . . And now so fascinated was he by his own meditations on this problem that he not only gazed and examined the plant and the fly, but proceeded to look about for other wonders. . . Then, after bending down and examining a blade of grass here, a climbing vine there, a minute flower, lovely and yet as inexplicable as his green fly, he turned in a kind of religious awe and wonder. Surely there must be a Creative Divinity, and so a purpose, behind all of this variety and beauty and tragedy of life. For see how tragedy had descended upon him, and still he had faith, and would have.[33]

Here we have Frank's squid and lobster all over again, but instead of skepticism as the conclusion, we get a statement of faith. We also get another example of the two-sidedness that occurs in so many aspects of Dreiser's life and work.

Dreiser's apparent determination to balance one character type against another is one way of accounting for *The Bulwark*; another way is to look to his background once again. Like other writers who derive from the Progressive era, Dreiser sensed that in the vicious business practices that had become common by 1900 could be seen the destruction of an admittedly naïve kind of economic idealism and an accompanying loss of innocence. His account of Solon's career is indicative of this attitude. Solon entered business with the belief that gaining and preserving property represented

the proper function and fruition of all lives. To accumulate or manage money in order to achieve good, or needed services, was a worthy and moral principle. For in the conserving of property, the rearing and education of children, and the helping of those not so fortunate or wise, one fell naturally in line with all Christian principles.

And since all Christian principles were of God, one also worshipped God by accumulating property and taking care of it in the best and most frugal and helpful way. It followed, as a matter of course, that great institutions were necessary in the service and care of money and property, and therefore those who served in them were more or less high priests of the people.[34]

But in the 1920s, at the end of his life, Solon realizes how outdated such reasoning has become. The accumulation of property does not fall in line with Christian principles so naturally; and the high priests of finance are, as often as not, robbers, not servants, of the people. It was a mistake to ever believe that the Quaker emphasis on simplicity could be reconciled with a banking career. Through Solon's life Dreiser demonstrates the impossibility of combining a moral stance with the amassing of riches, and in so doing points to a flaw in capitalist ideology.

The anti-capitalist sentiments that run through *The Bulwark* have been explained in terms of the social consciousness that Dreiser developed in the 1930s and that led to his joining the Communist Party in 1945. The philosophical conclusions in the book have similarly been ascribed to Dreiser's struggle, during the decade preceeding his death, with a long speculative work he intended to title *The Formulae Called Life* or *The Formula Called Man*. This work was never finished and now exists in eleven manuscript boxes of essays and newspaper clippings.[35] But neither explanation is necessary. The conclusions Dreiser comes to in *The Bulwark* are latent in his previous novels and can all be traced to his 1900-1920 period (especially the crucial midsection of those twenty-odd years). And it does not seem an exaggeration to suggest that *The Bulwark* is a rewrite of the *Trilogy*.

The real difference between *The Bulwark* and the *Trilogy* is stylistic, a difference that Granville Hicks effectively defines this way: "*The Bulwark* has all of the old clumsiness, but what is the essentially Dreiserian style is somehow exhibited in a purer vein than ever before. The writing is so commonplace that it becomes austere and even dignified. . . . for the most part the novel is written with a simplicity that begins by being annoying and ends by being impressive. Dreiser never told a story better than in *The Bulwark*."[36] While the latter point may be debated, Hicks's remarks on Dreiser's stylistic simplicity are exact. But then Dreiser's style always seems to be influenced by his subject matter. The sprawling sentences of the *Trilogy* are appropriate to the Cowperwood epic, just as the spareness of *The Bulwark* coincides with the emphasis on Quaker simplicity. The bareness of Solon's story extends to more than sentence structure, however; it is also evident in the lack of documentation—his financial career is barely detailed at all. Dreiser is almost too casual on this score, however, and gets his chronology mixed up (the 1920s he described is more like the pre-war years—his mention of dancers doing the two-step is but one example).

The Bulwark's stylistic peculiarities can be partially attributed to the editorial tossing-about it received before publication. When Dreiser finally got the manuscript together, he sent a copy to Louise Campbell, the woman who had helped edit *An American Tragedy*. She was not impressed with it and did not think it should be published in the form she had received it. Dreiser then asked James T. Farrell for his opinion. Farrell consulted with Mrs. Campbell and came up with some suggestions for revision. Dreiser passed the suggestions on to Donald B. Elder of Doubleday and

Co. Elder, after receiving further suggestions from
Mrs. Campbell, got the novel into final form. It was
published to bad reviews but sold well, earning $15,000
in royalties before the year was out and going through
a printing of 200,000 copies for the Book Find Club.

Those who found *The Bulwark* such an extraor-
dinary novel in style and structure could have looked
back to *Twelve Men,* another work whose genesis is
roughly that of the Quaker narrative. In *Twelve Men,*
a collection of sketches published in 1919 (most were
written much earlier) and a companion volume to the
later *A Gallery of Women,* Dreiser's sentimentality as
well as some of his leanest and most effective writing
are on display. These sketches range from a moving
portrait of Paul Dresser to an almost maudlin tribute
afforded a country doctor Dreiser knew when he was
a boy. Other memorable portraits include "A Doer of
the Word" (an understated account of Dreiser's con-
versation with "a contented man" in Noank, Connecti-
cut), "Culhane, the Solid Man" (Dreiser's impres-
sions of Muldoon, the physical culturist who ran the
health camp where Dreiser was sent to recover from
his crackup), and "The Village Feudists" (a strange
investigation of small-town rivalry). The style Dreiser
hits on in these pieces is well suited to telling anec-
dotes, and he achieves an easy verbal freedom that is
seldom evident in the novels.

Dreiser's curiosity and his powers of observation
are also factors contributing to the effectiveness of
Twelve Men. As in *A Gallery of Women,* Dreiser dis-
plays his tenacity in getting stories out of strange
people. Dreiser was never regarded as much of a talker,
but it is evident in his anecdotal writing that he was

a good listener and willing to ask the essential questions. Portions of *Twelve Men* show up in Dreiser's
novels ("The Mightly Rourke" in *The "Genius"* and
"Vanity, Vanity" in *The Stoic*) even though the collection is intended as little more than a notebook. Each
tale, some very suggestive of the peculiar pathos found
in Sherwood Anderson's stories, can be thought of as
a preface to an unwritten novel; but the strength of
the sketches is precisely that Dreiser did not draw them
out into novels. None of the portraits is quite concise,
but most are devoid of the roundabout tendency toward dogma that is a problem in all of Dreiser's longer
work, with the exception of *The Bulwark*.

Some of the same virtues can be seen, although
to a much lesser extent, in the volume of short stories,
Free, and Other Stories, Dreiser published in 1918.
Although some of the stories, such as "Will You Walk
Into My Parlor," are ruined by the unexpected ending
that was a dominant characteristic of the fiction in the
popular magazines of the day, others, including "Free"
and "The Second Choice," are remarkably effective.
"Free" is the story of a sixty-year-old architect who has
long wanted freedom from his wife. But when she
dies he is faced with the futility of his wish. "The
Second Choice" concerns a working-class girl who for-
gets the clerk she had intended to marry and falls in
love with a more appealing man, who is, however,
interested in her only briefly; abandoned, she finds herself forced to grimly put her life together again. Both
stories are cleanly told; but all-in-all, the book in which
they appear demonstrates Dreiser's limitations in that
genre, even though certain other stories, such as the
dreamily romantic "The Lost Phoebe," have received
considerable praise.

In addition to trying his hand at short-story writing, Dreiser gave playwriting a try. In the spring of 1913 he wrote his first one-acter, "The Girl in the Coffin." Five more plays followed in 1914. Dreiser thought he had a gift for the drama—and he did have some ability. "The Girl in the Coffin" was produced by the Washington Square Players with some success, but it is a contrived piece of theater. Labor leader William Magnet refuses to take part in a strike because his daughter has died while undergoing an abortion. The strike leader, John Ferguson, tells Magnet that the older man is not the only one to suffer loss. Ferguson's girl friend, whom he could not marry because he was already married, is also dead. Magnet is persuaded to forget his personal tragedy and become involved in the strike. Ferguson walks over to the coffin, and only then does the audience learn that Magnet's daughter and Ferguson's girl friend were the same person.

Almost all of Dreiser's plays concentrate on bizarre and often macabre incidents. "Laughing Gas," for instance, is something of an interior monologue set in an operating room as Jason James Vatabeel, a physician, undergoes a weird laughing-gas trip while having a tumor removed. The play illustrates, in a way that is all too obvious, Dreiser's theory of chemisms once again. This kind of illustration is typical of Dreiser's writing for the stage, and in "The Blue Sphere," "The Spring Recital," "In the Dark," "The Light in the Window," and " 'Old Ragpicker,' " many of his ideas can be seen dramatized in bare-bones fashion. The problem is that his plays are horrifying without being entertaining.

Dreiser's most important play, because of its relationship to *An American Tragedy*, is the full-length

drama *The Hand of the Potter*, which Dreiser worked
on in the fall of 1916. Isadore Berchansky, twenty-one,
comes from a poor family on New York's Lower East
Side. He is deformed physically and mentally, and he
has an uncontrollable desire for young girls. He attacks
and murders an eleven-year-old. Later he commits suicide, saying (and this statement is Dreiser's theme),
"It ain't my fault . . . I didn't make myself, did I?"[37]

The play deals with the complex questions of
guilt, justice, and mercy in a simplistic way. Dreiser
raises the question of who is to blame for what Isadore
is and does and proposes the old answer of chemisms,
environment, and a mysterious and obviously malicious
universal force that makes pawns of us all. In works
such as *The Hand of the Potter*, the aridity of some
of Dreiser's ideas and the unattractiveness of some aspects of his mind are overwhelming. Dreiser was to
deal with essentially the same ideas in *An American
Tragedy*, but the difference is that in the novel, through
characterization, piling up of detail, and establishing
a mood of oddly detached sympathy, he transforms
some elemental, almost naive ideas, into a powerful
aesthetic structure. Dreiser's magic as a writer is apparent when one compares these basically similar, ex-
tensively different, treatments of his most constant
leitmotif.

The Hand of the Potter was published in 1919
by Boni and Liveright. It was given an unsuccessful
production by the Provincetown Players that same
year.

The plays, along with the stories, *The "Genius,"*
the *Trilogy of Desire*, *The Bulwark*, and *Twelve Men*,
are part of the same phase in Dreiser's career, as dis-
jointed as publication dates make that phase appear.
All of these works were generated at approximately

the same time; and all, to varying degrees, of course, reflect a number of changes that came over Dreiser after 1910—the increased presence of his own personality and past in his books, a movement toward increased sentimentality, and a softening of the mood that permeates *Sister Carrie*, increasing social awareness, decreasing skepticism, and a tendency toward stylistic variation. An awareness of these changes does much to make the books that came out of this period understandable in relation to one another. But what is perhaps most important about these changes is that they indicate the solidification of artistic and intellectual qualities that went into *An American Tragedy*.

4

~~~~~~

Dreiser's
Explanation–
An American
Tragedy

I had long brooded upon the story, for it seemed to me not only to include every phase of our national life— politics, society, religion, business, sex—but it was a story so common to every boy reared in the smaller towns of America. It seemed so truly a story of what life does to the individual—and how impotent the individual is against such forces. My purpose was not to moralize— God forbid—but to give, if possible, a background and a psychology of reality which would somehow explain, if not condone, how such murders happen—and they have happened with surprising frequency in America as long as I can remember.

—*Letter to Jack Wilgus, April 20, 1927*

Explaining without moralizing—that is, in an essential way, the problem Dreiser faced as a novelist; and his ability to circumvent that problem is what made *Sister Carrie* such a shocking as well as genuinely innovative book. *An American Tragedy* is successful for the same reason, but in a much larger way, for in it Dreiser extends his abilities as a novelist and a thinker (given the definition suggested by the word *brooded*) farther than he was able to do before or after. His purpose in *An American Tragedy* is, on the face of it, both pretentious and ridiculous—to account for American politics, society, religion, business, and sex through a sensationalized narrative concerning the murder of a pregnant working girl and the subsequent trial of her lover, an ex-bellhop. But as Dreiser worked the story out, threading his way through the tangle of melodrama, subconscious symbolism, and the private obsessions of the public mind, he came up with something that, whatever its faults (lengthiness, dated vocabulary, silly dialogue), is an explanation of "how such murders happen" and why they happen so often in the United States. It is also, in a darker way than any of his other novels, an explanation of Dreiser himself.

While Dreiser began thinking about the type of crime around which *An American Tragedy* is structured as early as his St. Louis newspaper days, it was fortunate for him that the novel was not published until December, 1925. The 1920s are often thought of as a decade of frivolity, a time when, for the first time in America, fun was replacing the idea of duty. But the Twenties were "roaring" for another reason as well; it was the decade when the notion of the United States as a criminal society became almost matter-of-fact. At the top level were the gangs generated by Prohibition; newspapers of the time were full of stories

86

about gang wars, extortion, brutal machinegunnings. At the bottom level were the crimes of passion, poisonings, bludgeonings, drownings. It is more than coincidence that F. Scott Fitzgerald's *The Great Gatsby*, a story about a big-time bootlegger, should have appeared in the same year as Dreiser's story about a small-time murderer. Though very different stylistically, both these novels seek to deflate the American dream of success by showing how directly that dream is related to socially destructive acts.[1]

Oddly enough, Dreiser's attack on the American dream of success turned out to be in his only financially successful novel. He made almost $12,000 in royalties during the last two weeks of 1925 alone. A year later, the sales of the two-volume, five-dollar set had reached 50,000. The stage adaptation was grossing $30,000 a week in 1927, and Dreiser, as has been noted, sold the screen rights to Paramount's Famous Players for $90,000.

The novel was banned in Boston in April, 1927, and as a consequence sales elsewhere increased. As a publicity gimmick, Donald Friede of Boni and Liveright, Dreiser's publishers, went to Boston and got arrested for selling *An American Tragedy* to a police lieutenant. Boni and Liveright also sponsored a nationwide contest with a $500 prize for the best answer to the question of whether or not Dreiser's hero was guilty of first-degree murder. Given the sensation-seeking mood of the 1920s, Dreiser for once in his life was able to capitalize on public sentiment instead of merely scandalizing it.

However, topical interest in crime in 1925 differed considerably from that of Dreiser, who had long been fascinated by the kind of crime in which the killer is motivated by upward mobility. Matthiessen, in going through Dreiser's papers, found a file of newspaper clippings and copies of court records dealing with a variety of murder cases. Dreiser intended to write a novel based upon such material years before *An American Tragedy* was actually finished. Although most certainly not his first attempt at the topic, he wrote six chapters in 1919 about a 1911 case involving a minister who poisoned his pregnant girl friend because he was in love with a wealthy woman in his new parish. Dreiser then switched to a novel based on the story of Chester Gillette, who was a minor official in his uncle's skirt factory in Cortland, New York. His seduction of Grace Brown, a young mill-worker, had resulted in her pregnancy, but Chester had hopes of marrying the daughter of a local upper-class family. Soothing Grace's fears with promises of marriage, he took her to Big Moose Lake in the Adirondacks. He rented a boat and rowed Grace out onto the lake, where he stunned her with a tennis racket, tipped the boat over, and left her to drown as he swam ashore. Dreiser took note of this incident when it was reported in 1906, discussed it as the basis for a novel as early as 1907, and began work on it in 1920.

The book that resulted was one of the most difficult for Dreiser to write. He inspected the scene of the murder, examined the courtroom in which the Gillette trial was held, and even succeeded in getting permission to visit death row at Sing Sing. He consulted with an attorney and he discussed the psychology of murder with Dr. A. A. Brill, the psychiatrist who was Freud's official translator. In addition he met with the famous physiologist Dr. Jacques Loeb, whose studies in human response and instinct fitted in with Dreiser's analysis of the Gillette case. If anything, all of this made the novel harder to bring off. Dreiser often suffered from insomnia and he started to drink heavily. But he continued to write and rewrite, and the novel was announced for the fall of 1924. Dreiser, however, was not able to make the deadline, although he in fact overwrote. The manuscript at one point was over a million words long (compared to 385,000 in the finished version).

But when the novel at last came out, the delays necessitated by Dreiser's revision and extensions were unimportant in the face of the good reviews that began to appear in a wide range of newspapers and magazines. *The New York Sunday Times* printed a front-page review along with a photograph of Dreiser. The book was praised by Joseph Wood Krutch in *The Nation*, by Sherwood Anderson in the *Saturday Review*, and by Stuart Sherman in the *Herald Tribune*, although Mencken, never one to run to pattern, gave it a negative notice in the *American Mercury*. The critics generally realized what Gerber later pointed out, that "Had the fates granted Dreiser but a single novel in which to dramatize the beliefs and lessons of his lifetime, that volume would of necessity have been *An American Tragedy*."[2] They also realized that in the characterization Dreiser gives his hero, Clyde Griffiths, he indicts American society in a way no other writer up to that time had done.

"Plainly there was something wrong somewhere,"[3] young Clyde Griffiths thinks as he considers the puzzling contradiction between what his streetcorner evangelist parents expect their religion to do for them and what it actually does do. "How Sweet the Balm of Jesus' Love" is the hymn Clyde's mother asks her family to sing as they stand on a Kansas City sidewalk at the start of *An American Tragedy*; but Clyde, contemplating the shabby clothing he must wear, the storefront mission in which he must live, and the taunts he receives from other boys his age, does not perceive much sweetness. This contrast between the expectations of his parents, who represent the naïve tradition of evangelicalism in American life (a tradition that had its manifestations in the 1920s in Billy Sunday revivalism, gospel missions, and fundamentalism of the sort made famous in the 1925 Scopes Monkey Trial), and the disappointments of Clyde, who represents the twentieth-century materialistic impulse, continues throughout the rest of the book. Clyde is influenced by his parents' idealism, but he cannot get things straight, cannot understand sacrifice of the sort he is asked to make. Furthermore, according to Dreiser, Clyde "was one of those interesting individuals who looked upon himself as a thing apart—never quite wholly and indissolubly merged with the family of which he was a member, and never with any profound obligations to those who had been responsible for his coming into the world."[4]

So by the time Clyde is 16, awakened to sex and obsessed with fine clothes, houses, watches, rings, and other benefits that would never come to him if he followed his parents' example, he has already rejected his background. He gets a job in a drugstore and then a much better job as a bellhop at the Green-Davidson Hotel with the chance to make twenty-five dollars a week or more. And here the grim retelling of the Horatio Alger plot so favored by Dreiser begins.

Clyde's fortunes improve; but as they do, the distance between him and his parents increases. He lies to his mother about his actual income in order to avoid turning over to his impoverished family money that could be spent on his own pleasure. And when his sister Esta, who has run away with an actor, comes back to Kansas City pregnant, Clyde does not provide as much money as he could to help her. He holds the cash back because he has agreed to help his girl friend, Hortense Briggs, buy a fur coat. Hortense, a vain, stupid girl, is using Clyde and he knows it; but he cannot bring himself to give her up. Nor can he resist the pleasure of roistering about with the other bellhops and their girl friends. He is fast caught up in the easily accessible pleasures offered by the 1920s economy of abundance. "We . . . feel, in this book, the burden of a historical moment," Warren writes, "the moment of the Great Boom, which climaxed the period from Grant to Coolidge, the half-century in which the new America of industry and finance capitalism was hardening into shape and its secret forces were emerging to dominate all life."[5] Given Clyde's sensuous nature and the allurements offered by the Great Boom, the influence of his parents' Christianity is all but lost on him.

But the snares and the pitfalls Clyde's preacher father had warned him against are real, even if the love of Jesus might not be. Returning from a midwinter outing in a borrowed car, Clyde and his friends run over a little girl. They try to get away, but the car overturns. Clyde, even though he was not driving, fears involvement with the law. He escapes across a field, away from his Kansas City days and his round of good times.

After a period of wandering from city to city and from job to job, Clyde winds up as a bellhop at the Union League Club in Chicago. There he luckily encounters his rich uncle Samuel Griffiths, owner of the Griffiths Collar and Shirt Company, of Lycurgus, New York. Uncle Samuel is impressed with Clyde's

appearance and his seeming earnestness—so impressed
that Clyde is brought to Lycurgus and put to work in
the lower reaches of the factory so that he will be
able to learn the business from the ground up. Already
Dreiser has touched on two American folktales: the
fast crowd and the rich uncle. He is soon to touch on
others.

Some months pass and Clyde (against the jealous
objections of his look-alike cousin Gilbert, who resents
his father's interest in Clyde) is placed in charge of a
room full of girls who are employed in stamping size
numbers on collars. He is given a strong warning about
entering into romantic involvements with the girls in
his section. Such relationships would betray the confidence his uncle has placed in him and would mean
the end of his career. But Clyde, Dreiser hero that
he is, cannot resist becoming interested in Roberta
Alden, a country girl with a background of poverty
and frustration not unlike Clyde's own—or Sister Carrie's for that matter. Roberta falls in love with Clyde
(to her he is an important person, her boss and a
Griffiths, a good catch) and eventually the worst
happens: she gets pregnant. Two more myths are thus
brought into the story: that of the seduced country
girl (although who seduces whom is an open question)
and that of the promising youth whose career is destroyed through the consequences of sexual involvement.

Clyde has in the meantime fallen in love with
Sondra Finch, daughter of a wealthy Lycurgus family.
He thinks that she may marry him; if she does, his
future will be assured. His dream, a male version of
the one Roberta has of him, is to marry both money
and beauty. And this dream constitutes the basis of
another folktale.

What is Clyde to do? He no longer loves Roberta and he knows that if he marries her he faces the loss of his job, rejection by his newly-found rich relatives, and a lifetime of unhappiness. He tries to help Roberta abort the baby, but they can find no medicine that will work, and without a lot of money or influence a surgical abortion is impossible to arrange. At the same time Clyde is unable to break away from Sondra and the high-society crowd of which he has become a shirttail member. For a while he is unable to do anything about his dilemma, until he reads one day of a mysterious drowning at Pass Lake in Massachusetts. A boat, rented by a young man and a woman, was found overturned, two hats floating nearby. The body of the woman was recovered but not that of the man. A very unoriginal plan begins to form in Clyde's brain.

But can he carry it out? Can he actually murder Roberta? He is not sure, but he makes arrangements for her to go with him to Grass Lake for a premarital honeymoon. The area, however, is too crowded for his purpose, so he persuades Roberta to accompany him to another, more isolated lake, Big Bittern. They rent a boat and row to the far end of the lake, but he finds that his will is strangely paralyzed. He sits with his camera in his hands, Roberta expecting him to take more pictures of her as he said he would. The boat drifts, and yet he cannot move.

Roberta, worried by the strange look on Clyde's face, starts toward him in the boat. A wave of repulsion passes over him; he does not want her to touch him and pushes out at her with the camera. As she is struck, she screams; Clyde is so startled that he lurches forward to help her and inadvertently capsizes the boat. Roberta is hit on the head by a gunwale as she sinks. She surfaces and cries for help. What Clyde

lacked the nerve to carry out has happened by accident. Again, he does not act, and the water closes
over Roberta.

Clyde swims to the place on shore where he had
earlier left his bag. He hides the camera tripod that
he had strapped to his gear (the camera has gone into
the lake) and heads south through the woods. Although he accidentally encounters three woodmen, his
escape is uneventful and he is able to make his way
to the not-so-distant summer place of Sondra's family
friends, the Cranstons. There, with many disturbing
thoughts about the accident, he falls back into the
round of tennis, picnics, canoeing, and lovemaking to
which Roberta's pregnancy had been such a threat.

Given the amateurish way Clyde has carried out
his plot, there is no chance of his not being found out.
The camera and tripod are found and traced to Clyde.
A search of Roberta's possessions and information obtained from her parents turns up evidence linking her
to Clyde. A warrant is obtained to enter Clyde's room
in Lycurgus, and there the pleading letters Roberta had
written concerning her pregnancy are discovered. A
warrant is issued for Clyde's arrest, and he is appre-
hended in the woods back of the campsite he and
Sondra were enjoying with their friends. Taken to the
Cataraqui County jail to await trial, he is no longer
the Horatio Alger hero; now he is the society boy who
has slain a poor working girl—or so the newspapers
categorize him.

A sensational trial will develop, and ready to take
advantage of it is Orville W. Mason, the district attorney. His own life, just as Clyde's did until Orville
entered it, illustrates a venerable American success
story. The son of a poor widow, Mason became a reporter, then read law, was admitted to the bar, and

began to make his way up the ladder of local politics. He has his eye on the Republican nomination for the county judgeship, and he knows that the attention Clyde's trial will inevitably attract might also win some votes. Mason is as much of an opportunist as Clyde, but there is an important difference; a teenage accident has disfigured Mason's face, leaving what Dreiser calls a "psychic sex scar."[6] Jealousy of Clyde's good looks and success with girls thus partly motivates Mason, but he is played up by the newspapers as the vigorous, fighting D.A., a man determined to protect the public from criminals. Through this public image of Mason, Dreiser sets another myth going.

Clyde's attorneys, Alvin Belknap and Reuben Jephson, hired by the Griffiths family, are Democrats and consequently are willing to take Clyde on so that Mason's political ambitions might be thwarted. They are also willing to change Clyde's story so that he will have a better chance with the jury. Ironically, Clyde, the person on trial, is not the central issue in it. The trial becomes a political confrontation and a public spectacle as it drags on for weeks. The evidence against Clyde is overwhelming, even though the question of guilt is so complex that not even Clyde is certain about whether or not he actually murdered Roberta. As things turn out, he does not have a chance; the jury convicts him of murder in the first degree, and he is sentenced to the electric chair.

But two more twisted melodramas are yet to be acted out. Clyde's mother comes to visit him in the state prison, her journey being paid for by a Denver newspaper to which she is to send dispatches describing her reunion with Clyde (this detail is one of the grossest indictments of American crassness to be found in Dreiser). Mrs. Griffiths canvasses the local churches

to raise funds for a new trial after she learns that the
Griffiths of Lycurgus have decided that further support of Clyde would be a waste of money. She has
little success and at last is forced to go back to Denver,
although later on she is able to return to Clyde. She
leaves him in the care of the Rev. Duncan McMillan
of Syracuse, who visits him repeatedly, hoping that
Clyde will repent and turn to Jesus. But as in the
beginning of his story, Clyde cannot get straight in
his mind how he feels about religion. Just as he could
neither act to drown Roberta as he had planned, nor
act to save her, and just as he cannot decide about
his own guilt, so he cannot make up his mind about
Rev. McMillan's message. Finally, in the days before
his execution, and driven by "a kind of psychic terror,"[7]
he composes a last message, addressed especially to
other young men of his age and inclinations, a message
in which he testifies to having accepted Christ as his
personal savior. The letter goes out, but the story the
world receives about Clyde's death-house conversion,
like everything they have read about him in the newspapers, is not quite true.

All appeals fail, including a personal visit by Mrs.
Griffiths to the governor, and Clyde makes his last
walk. "Now it was here," Dreiser writes; "now it was
being opened. There it was—at last—the chair he had
so often seen in his dreams. . . He was being pushed
toward that—into that—on—on—through the door
which was now open—to receive him—but which was
as quickly closed again on all the earthly life he had
ever known."[8]

And so Clyde's tragedy ends, leaving many readers
to wonder just what is American about it and if it is
indeed a tragedy. The word *American* can be easily

justified in several ways. First, the word was used in the titles of dozens of books during the wave of self-criticism and nationalistic awareness that swept over the United States after World War I.[9] And second, as Matthiessen emphasizes, "Dreiser's central thought in putting the word American into his title was the overwhelming lure of money-values in our society, more nakedly apparent than in older and more complex social structures."[10] But *Tragedy* is another matter, and many critics would agree with the notion that the novel "contains no single element of tragedy in any legitimate sense of the word, and it impresses thoughtful readers as a mere sensational newspaper story long drawn out."[11]

Dreiser, of course, does not present a tragic story in the classic sense; instead, he gives us, as Warren points out, a tragedy with "the lowest common denominator of tragic effect."[12] This reduction in itself, making not a king but a factory straw boss the hero, makes it possible to account for the book as a tragic form suitable for the world's greatest democracy. But how much of a reduction is it? Clyde is indecisive like Hamlet. Like Lear he is blind to his own self. And like Othello he is uncertain of his own self-definition. He goes to his death not knowing who he is, finding no home—even after wandering across half of the continent. Like all tragic heroes his fight ultimately must be seen as the struggle against the illusions Dreiser attacks: wealth, power, love, and, most tragically, the self.

But Clyde's tragedy must be looked at in another perspective because of the way so many American assumptions—the melodramatic myths that wind through the narrative—are controverted by Dreiser. It is not simply a matter of the Horatio Alger plot being turned

around; nor is it simply a matter of the ironic twists
Dreiser gives the story of the country girl, the story of
the fighting D.A., the story of the convict's mother,
or the story of salvation on death row. It is instead
Dreiser's invitation to consider these stories, in the
manner they are usually told, as solutions for the ills in
American life. The American tragedy, suggests Dreiser,
is believing in solutions of the sort he attacks; indeed,
is believing in solutions at all.

The popular American outlook is essentially comic,
the belief that no matter how complex, how unfortunate a dilemma, a solution is always possible. If
Clyde's parents are poor, he can get a job and make
something of himself. If he falls into bad company
and gets into trouble, he can always make a new start
elsewhere, and if he behaves himself in his new life,
maybe Lady Luck will smile on him—maybe his rich
uncle will help him out. If he makes another mistake
and his girl friend gets pregnant and he really is in
love with someone else, there must be a solution. And
so it goes, until Clyde goes too far in seeking solutions.
But even after the murder, even after he is arrested
and brought to trial, there is the hope that his lawyers
can get him off. If he is convicted, perhaps his case
can be appealed. And if, at last, he must die, there is
still Jesus. One solution after another, but for Clyde
no solutions at all. One definition of tragedy is that
it is the acceptance of the reality of there being no
solutions, and only when we realize there is no way
out for Clyde do we understand his tragedy. Appro-
priately enough, one of the most tragic aspects of the
story is Clyde's comic readiness to believe in solutions,
but then his story is *an* American tragedy.

Compounding the tragedy is the foolishness of
Clyde's hopefulness. Had he remained a bellhop, he

would have had no future; but because of his cousin Gilbert's jealousy, Clyde's future in the factory is not exactly bright. His career is bound to end with old Mr. Griffith's death or retirement. Clyde dreams of marrying Sondra and being taken into her father's business, thus escaping Gilbert's power. But this too is an unsound hope. Sondra herself is reluctant to discuss marriage and her parents are wary of Clyde. In all of the solutions that Clyde thinks are before him at various times, he is deceived. Like Oedipus he labors under delusion, although he does not enjoy the same noble fate as his painfully symbolic drama draws to an end.

For much of the deeply suggestive effect Dreiser achieves in *An American Tragedy*, he relies on the same kind of subconscious symbolism found in *Sister Carrie*. Clyde is in a canoe when he first encounters Roberta outside of the factory room. Later, when he rows her out onto Big Bittern Lake he falls into a trance like Thoreau on Walden Pond.[13] And after the drowning he makes his escape through woods. These symbols, the canoe, the lake, the woods, all so intricately involved in Clyde's tragedy, are distinctly American symbols and function to give the novel its dream-like quality, as do other symbols that are not quite so deeply embedded in American literature. Clyde is attracted by the bright lights of the city, and it is his longing for the kind of excitement that those lights emblazon that accounts for his presence in the car in Kansas City (even though he is returning from an excursion in the country) when the little girl is run over. Years later, when he is sitting on death row, he sees the prison lights dim when his rowmates are executed one by one.

The hotels in which Clyde works become, in a way, a metaphor of his life. He is doomed to be a transient, moving from room to room, never finding any permanence, and never traveling first-class himself. He is an American type, forever on the move—until he is caught (and even then, like Daniel Boone, he is wishing he could disappear into the wilderness).

Even the collar factory is symbolic. Uncle Samuel in putting Clyde to work is seeing if his nephew can wear the collar of responsibility. Roberta, when she gets pregnant, tries to put the collar of marriage on Clyde. And Orville Mason, when he is convinced that Clyde is a murderer, simply wants to collar him. But as subterranean as any of these symbols is Dreiser's use once again of the door. The death-chamber door contrasts with the "Door of Hope Mission" Clyde's mother runs—a contrast reminiscent of the safe door and the door of Hurstwood's suicide room in *Sister Carrie*.

Just as the popular myths crisscross in *An American Tragedy*, so too do the symbols form a current that runs beneath the surface of Dreiser's narrative. One is hesitant to claim that the mythic or the symbolic structure of the novel were carefully planned by Dreiser (the pieces fit together only roughly). Instead, Dreiser was so attuned to the murmurings and cravings that are a part of what is called, for lack of a better term, the popular mind, that these aspects of the book seem to be there by instinct.

This, of course, does not account for the entire symbolic structure of the novel, which is often not all that dark or deep. The novel opens and ends with street preaching scenes that, in a conscious and obvious way, underscores the conflict between materialism and religious idealism that is part of Dreiser's tragic concept in his musings about American culture.

Another use of transparent symbolism occurs in the death-row section of the novel when Nicholson, a lawyer who had been convicted of poisoning a client to gain control of his estate, gives Clyde two books— *Robinson Crusoe* and the *Arabian Nights*. Clyde is like Crusoe in that he too is isolated, but ironically is forced to fall back on a self that is anything but reliant. And like Aladdin in the *Arabian Nights*, Clyde is bewitched by beauty, love, and wealth; Dreiser is careful to emphasize the comparison by describing the opportunities offered by the Green-Davidson Hotel as "Aladdinish" and by having a genii-like voice urge Clyde to act as Roberta cries for help.[14] And then there is Dreiser's employment of the "double" to give the reader contrasting images of Clyde's personality and predicament.[15] Not only does Clyde have an interior voice—his other self—tempting him and cautioning him, he has his cousin Gilbert, who looks so much like Clyde that the two are often mistaken for one another. Gilbert, in his jealousy and arrogance, is Clyde had Clyde been given the same background. The same could be said of Clyde's other double, Orville Mason, who has Clyde's background of poverty but who drives himself to succeed because of his psychic sex scar. One of the most ironic developments in the novel is that Clyde should be successfully prosecuted by his own double; but then Clyde, in his congenital confusion, repeatedly double-crosses himself and his story becomes, like Camus's *The Stranger*, another "portrait of twentieth-century man as the victim of his own crime."[16]

Dreiser's portrait of Clyde is, of course, something of a portrait of Dreiser himself. Dreiser had many second thoughts about his own marriage, as *The "Genius"* so thoroughly documents, and it takes no psychiatrist to see an image of the first Mrs. Dreiser in Roberta, although a comparison of the two women is unfair. But the relationship between Clyde and his creator is much more subtle than the obvious level of wish-fulfillment in the novel indicates. Dreiser as a youth had many of Clyde's materialistic longings, and it was not until *An American Tragedy* came out that those longings were adequately fulfilled. More hauntingly, as a boy Dreiser had a traumatic experience that is transformed into the central event in the book.

His wastrel brother Rome took young Dreiser out in a boat on the Wabash River and cruelly rocked it back and forth. Dreiser told this story, with considerable variation, many times, long remembering the appearance of the water—"mysterious, ominous and most uncertain"—and saying that ever after "I could not view any considerable body of water without having brought back to me most clearly that particular sensation of something that could and might destroy me, and that with almost personal violence."[17] Dreiser was terrified—terror that later was transferred to Roberta's face. Just as Roberta, given her origins, is another of Clyde's doubles, so she is also an image of Dreiser.

Dreiser's manner of working reflections of himself, ironic melodrama, and unconscious and consciously devised symbolism into his fiction results in a novel that resembles one of its own metaphors—the dark waters of Big Bittern Lake. *An American Tragedy* has a turgid quality that offends some readers but pleases others. Whatever the effect, this quality is one of Dreiser's unique achievements as a writer. Despite the problems with his prose[18]—the archaisms, faulty idiom, unfortunate coinages, dangling modifiers, failures in agreement, and the distressing tendency to have his lovers converse in baby talk—Dreiser combines narrative elements and chains of imagery that produce what Warren has called "the movie in our heads,"[19] an unforgettable progress of unfolding scenes. It is this rather than the social criticism that stays with us even if Dreiser is basically concerned with pointing out that "Emersonian self-reliance had been perverted by predators into an astonishing complacency and indifference to the moving course of history."[20] Such a critical pronouncement is true and valuable, but not quite adequate in accounting for what it is Dreiser does in *An American Tragedy*. Oddly enough, for that we must look at Dreiser in terms of technique, even though he is usually thought of as a novelist of ideas, a writer who wanted to use the novel as a vehicle for philosophy.

Dreiser's artistry is difficult to discuss because so much of it must be attributed to natural tendencies. Certainly it is Dreiser's natural tendency to let his dark symbols float and to draw his narrative out that works to his advantage in *An American Tragedy*. Where in *The Financier* the long section devoted to Frank's trial serves only a slight purpose aesthetically, in *An American Tragedy* the drawing-out of Clyde's trial becomes, finally, a superbly masterful treatment of suspense. The lengthiness of the trial section also corresponds to the lengthy deliberations Clyde goes through in deciding what he is going to do about Roberta. It is structurally fitting that as much space be given to the legal decision eventually made concerning Clyde's crime as Clyde gave to his own agonizing meditation over whether or not to commit the crime. Despite the many negative things that must be said about the way Dreiser handles the form of his

other novels, his technique, his style, and the essentially sentimental power of his imagination work together to produce in *An American Tragedy* a narrative
that is at once a folk-epic and a complex work of
something other than art—a "psychology of reality,"
perhaps.

5

Dreiser's

Philosophy

and Politics

Not to cling too pathetically to a religion or a system of government or a theory of morals or a method of living, but to be ready to abandon at a moment's notice is the apparent teaching of the ages—to be able to step out free and willing to accept new and radically different conditions.

—*Hey, Rub-A-Dub-Dub!*

The scene at the end of The "Genius" in which Eugene Witla walks out onto his yard one November night and looks up into endless space is emblematic of Dreiser's self-image. Dreiser thought of himself as a thinker, a brooder not only upon silences but also upon the whole welter of life. He was, in one sense, ill-prepared for such a task; he was poorly educated, his reading was erratic, and he often came to weighty conclusions without realizing that, despite their weight, they are the substance of clichés. As Mencken wrote in a letter to Burton Rascoe, "Dreiser is a great artist, but a very ignorant and credulous man. He believes, for example in the Ouija board."[1] Yet in another sense despite his tendency toward superstition (Dreiser liked to consult fortunetellers, he worried over omens, and he did believe in the Ouija board) and a certain failure to realize the limitations forced upon him by his intellectual background, Dreiser's curiosity along with his compassion for the unfortunate made it possible for him to achieve reflective moments in his novels that sometimes suggest Melville, Dostoevsky, and Tolstoy. Moreover, Dreiser's compulsive brooding had manifestations outside of his fiction, especially in two often-neglected aspects of his life—his philosophic writing and his political involvement.

It is, of course, inexact to term Dreiser a philosopher. He had little training in the modes of formal philosophical discourse, and a logician would be able to read Dreiser's ruminative essays only with considerable irritation. As in his novels, Dreiser often writes too much and says too little, but in the one philosophic volume he published, Hey, Rub-a-Dub-Dub!, there are, along with many inconsistencies and much triteness, dozens of striking sentences, moods that are frequently

106

charming, and reflections that occasionally make aspects of Dreiser's novels more understandable.

Hey, Rub-A-Dub-Dub!, which came out in March,
1920, is subtitled "A Book of the Mystery and Wonder
and Terror of Life." The title and the subtitle suggest
the sort of conflict present throughout Dreiser's
thought. Dreiser explained the title by saying that it,
like life itself, has no meaning. And this attitude is
just what a superficial interpretation of Dreiser's writing would support. The subtitle, on the other hand,
brings out another side of Dreiser—his deep involvement with the mysterious, with chemical relationships,
dreams, the vagaries of human personality, crime and
punishment, the meaning of sexuality, the courses of
the stars. The appeal of Dreiser's essays—like that of
his novels—is not in his pronouncements on life's ultimate blankness, but in his ability to ponder life's
mystery, wonder, and terror. Those familiar with
Dreiser's fiction are not surprised that in these essays
his pondering seldom reaches a point of decisive pronouncement. Dreiser broods, and he wonders, but like
his Clyde Griffiths he always stops short of figuring
things out; he remains unconvinced, open-minded.

Dreiser's philosophic view emerges in the first (and
title) essay in *Hey, Rub-A-Dub-Dub!* In this essay he
assumes a persona, one John Paradiso (the name taken
from Dreiser's first employer in Chicago), who is living
in an impoverished New Jersey neighborhood in sight
of the Woolworth Building across the river. At once
the contrast between the splendid and the wretched
that is so prevalent in Dreiser's work is apparent. On
one side of the river is a fabled city of riches, its very
existence seeming to mock those on the other side, the
poor, the stupid, the deformed. Or else it lures them

across with the great myth: "Turn the pages of any magazine—are there not advertisements of and treatises on How To Be Successful, with the authors thereof offering to impart their knowledge of how so to be for a comparative song?"[2] Paradiso sees through the myth of success, just as he sees through whatever his eyes behold; he fails to discern much evidence of Divine Mind or Truth or Justice in anything. He gives some depressing cases in point, all gleaned from the newspapers—old people who die while waiting in line for bundles of cast-off clothing, an attendant in an Odd Fellows Home chloroforming his patients because he was tired of them, a well-known charity spending $150,000 on running expenses and only $90,000 on actual relief, a man serving twenty years for a crime he was later discovered not to have committed, etc.

Paradiso offers no explanations for why such things should happen. To him the world is "topsy-turvy . . . impossible of a fixed explanation or rule."[3] The world, man, animals, insects—all seem, despite the beauty and delight that is nonetheless often present, without aim and of no use. This is not necessarily bad, for after all it is the chaos in life that is exciting, the ambiguity that makes art possible. While he does not understand life, Paradiso nonetheless likes it: "Plainly it produces all the fine spectacles I see."[4] What is most deplorable, he thinks, is not the confusion and injustice that is present all around. After all, perhaps we cannot do anything about essential conditions. But what we can do is to avoid holding to systems of belief and morality that fail to take into account the inconsistency, the cruelty, and the random nature of life as it can be observed daily by any dispassionate onlooker. Paradiso's own observations and experiences lead to the conclusion that "there is scarcely a so-called 'sane,' right, merciful, true, just, solution to anything."[5] This skepticism is, of course, Dreiser's central attitude. He is, in the words of Paradiso, "one of those curious persons who cannot make up their minds about any-thing."[6]

The eagerness to find and accept solutions is at-tacked again and again in Dreiser's novels and essays because it is, for him, a failure of nerve. To survive, as John Paradiso does, amid the pressures of confusion, being reminded everytime he opens a newspaper of the horror that is daily present in thousands of flesh-and-blood tragedies, and still not give himself over to illusion—that, for Dreiser, is true heroism. But the fact that there are no solutions does not mean that one should turn away from the mysteries of life. Solutions destroy mystery, and this is why Dreiser was so hesitant to believe in any of them. He wanted to sit and wonder about things, as Paradiso does at the end of the first essay: "Yet here is the great river—that is beautiful; and Mr. Woolworth's tower, a strange attempt on the part of man to seem more than he is; and a thousand other evidences of hopes and dreams, all too frail per-haps against the endless drag toward nothingness, but still lovely and comforting. And yet. . . ."[7] Dreiser's thinking always leads on toward the "And yet," toward the reconciliation, not of opposites exactly, nor of contradiction, but of one reality with another, one idea with another, one bit of experience with another.

The subsequent chapters of *Hey, Rub-a-Dub-Dub!* (including three all but unreadable plays), while re-turning to the theme of illusion again and again, move Dreiser's philosophy toward comprehensiveness in out-line if not in fact. One by one he considers such topics as the principle of change in the universe, man's place in nature, the makeup of the human personality, the

importance of the sex impulse, the psychological consequences of manual labor, marriage and divorce, and
the idea of progress. Although Dreiser does not stick
to a chapter-by-chapter development of his thought,
it is possible to put together a synthesis of his ideas,
keeping in mind that in Dreiser's thinking there are
no conclusions, only the belief that "Not to cling too
pathetically to a religion or a system of government or
a theory of morals or a method of living, but to be
ready to abandon at a moment's notice is the apparent
teaching of the ages—to be able to step out free and
willing to accept new and radically different conditions."[8]

This is the best state for the human mind, Dreiser
argues, because in nature nothing is fixed and every
individual is part of a vast restlessness. When we make
up rules, such as those governing marriage, we fly in
the face of external flux and only contribute to our
own unhappiness. As a consequence, man's place in
nature is severely limited—and even more severely limited if he continues to view nature in terms of rigid
and illusory symptoms, such as the idea that each man
possesses the potentialities of greatness: "If Nature
wishes one to rise above the conditions wherewith he
finds himself surrounded at birth She usually provides
him with the equipment for so doing during gestation,
or before, and in addition accidental and most oppor-
tune circumstances invariably aid him. . . Vide Caesar,
Napoleon, Shakespeare, Luther, Lincoln, even Goethe."[9]
Personality is determined long before birth and all life
can do is to provide the opportunity for inherent capacities to develop within the scheme of universal
and quite likely undirected change.

The development of these capacities is overwhelm-
ingly influenced, however, by sexual drives that provide

the major evidence for a chemical theory of human makeup. Unfortunately, human societies have organized themselves again and again to suppress or even ignore this dominant aspect of motivation, and the result (in the United States especially) is neurosis. "The truth no doubt is," Dreiser writes about sexuality, "that in this much-maligned impulse which chemical forces beyond and above the willing of men are compounding lies the destiny of man (if he has one), only we are not as yet able to fathom that destiny. Here we come, bottles of fluid dynamite (prepared by what satiric super-soul and why?) and somewhere in the world is, or may be, another compound which will set us aflame—and we are supposed to connect this with a narrow religious order or theory!"[10]

Dreiser projects an image of secretive, mysterious Nature, seemingly indifferent to man's haphazard and fumbling progress (if progress it is), yet his Nature is a force or presence that seemingly abides by a principle of "swing," or balance—for every action there is a reaction, a condition of checks and balances—that Dreiser terms the "equation Inevitable." We are chemical beings, but "Nature has supplied us with certain forces and chemic tendencies and responses, and has also provided (rather roughly in certain instances) the checks and balances which govern the same."[11] We are the victims of constant change, but change that can go only so far in one direction before an opposing force appears as a corrective.

Life is often painful, but we are physically prevented from suffering pain beyond a certain point. And it is here, in this equational conception of Nature, that an essential point concerning Dreiser's thinking is often missed—that his skepticism very readily turns into a tempered form of optimism: "Life is as it is—

active, dancing, changeful, beautiful, at once brutal and
tender—regardless of how our theories would seek to
make it seem, and though it does as it chooses at times,
or appears to, and invents or assumes various guises of
perfection, it is as it always has been, both good and
bad, yet held in a kind of equational vise or harmony
—neither too good nor too bad—or we would not be
here at all, any of us, to tell the tale."[12] Man's plight
may be essentially tragic—he is a nonentity *and* aware
of it—but out of the equational vise he is able to
synthesize not only art but a reasonable idea of divinity: "Our God is tragedy and comedy, terror and delight . . . limitless opportunity and endless opposition
and destruction, for His way is extremes in equation,
and nothing more and nothing less."[13] This is not exactly a positive view, but neither is it the grim mechanism of despair often credited to Dreiser.

His reflections on "Nature," particularly in the
essay "The Reformer," but in many other chapters of
Hey, Rub-a-Dub-Dub!, have an oddly Emersonian, if
not exactly transcendental quality to them. Nature, to
Dreiser, is thought of in relationship to pervading goodness; but he is not willing to give a conception of evil
the upper hand either. To him Nature is wise, avoid-
ing median conditions or strict balances between opposite forces because this would be nothingness. "Her
mood," Dreiser writes, "if anything is synchronic, rhyth-
mic, pendulumic. She wishes, if one may interpret Her
wishes from what may be seen here, to swing in a
semi-balanced way between extremes of so-called good
and evil—never all good and never all evil, but a little
of both, or plenty, in order that there may be con-
tention, strife, something to live *about* and for."[14] Nature may not always seem kind to us, but it is not bad.
What we really need, Dreiser emphasizes, "is a better

stomach for life as it is, and Nature, in the course of time, may possibly build us such."[15]

When we follow Dreiser's reasoning to its inevitable conclusions, we see that he is, like his near contemporary Hardy, something of a meliorist. This tendency is present in Dreiser's novels, even though none of them, not even *The Bulwark*, can be said to have a happy ending. Dreiser's "happier" characters—Carrie, Jennie, Eugene, Solon, and, not to be overlooked, John Paradiso—all learn how to stomach Nature and the eternal swing of forces. Others, Clyde Griffiths certainly, and Frank Cowperwood to a certain extent, are struck down by the pendulum. But all of these characters have a place in Dreiser's peculiar scheme of things, a scheme that is not mechanistic, naturalistic, Freudian, or behavioristic, although it involves related and often derivative ideas. Dreiser's philosophy is a partly scientific, partly mystic collection of thoughts that come out of his emotions as much as his intellect; its roots are in American Transcendentalism, the tough line of the Darwinians, the compassionate response of the Progressive era, and his own turn-of-the-century conglomeration of experience.

This is certainly borne out in the long, unfinished, and unpublished philosophical volume Dreiser worked on for years. Variously titled *The Mechanism Called Man*, *The Formulae Called Life*, and *The Formula Called Man*, Dreiser's treatise was, according to one plan, to consist of forty chapters, beginning with an essay on the universe, its origin and meaning, and ending with a chapter on the problem of death. Dreiser gathered material for this project by going on occasional scientific and philosophical kicks, studying experimental biology, physics, and applied mechanics; he also visited numerous laboratories and observatories. His interest in this work was at its peak in 1934–35, when depressed by a long period of ill health he felt impelled to set his mind in order. Though Dreiser was excited over his book of ruminations, his obsession with the work dismayed his publisher and many of his friends, most of whom thought he would be far better off devoting his time to another novel.

His enthusiasm for his *Mechanism* or *Formula* book was dampened somewhat in 1935 when hundreds of pages of notes were damaged in a downpour through which he and Helen drove in Arkansas. Although until his death he continued to think about developing a definitive statement of his thought, he was never able to pull his materials together, which is perhaps just as well. What remains of this proposed major work indicates that Dreiser would have given us little that was new. His notes do show, however, an increasing tendency toward mysticism, or at least toward a softer view of things that eventually shows up in *The Bulwark*.

The melioristic turn in Dreiser's thought also explains his seemingly sudden interest in political theories after the publication of *An American Tragedy*. The standard conception of Dreiser as a despairing mechanist makes his direct involvement in social reform and his membership in the Communist Party appear at best contradictory, at worst intellectually dishonest. But Dreiser's inconsistency on this point is diminished considerably when one realizes that he increasingly came to blame social injustice on rigid political and economic attitudes and illusory conceptions of Nature's pendulumic swing. And it must be emphasized that Dreiser's thinking on these matters is not a consequence of either the attention focused on him by the success of *An American Tragedy* or of the awak-

ened social consciousness that affected so many other
writers in the late 1920s. Two essays in *Hey, Rub-A-
Dub-Dub!*—"Some Aspects of Our National Character," and "More Democracy or Less? An Inquiry"—
show that Dreiser's development as a pamphleteer on
matters of national concern was not sudden or late.

In these essays Dreiser attacks American democracy as an illusion. The United States, given the en-
thusiasms of our founding ideologists, was to be a
place of intellectual and spiritual freedom: "Our children and our children's children were to be free, progressive, fearless, mentally and spiritually alert, entirely
loosened from the trammels and chains of superstition
and the degradation of poverty and want."[16] But this
idea of democracy is an unrealized dream, Dreiser argues. Instead of freedom there is repression; and the
chains of superstition and poverty still bind. The wealth
is controlled by a small percentage of the population;
the poor are taken advantage of and lied to; and we
are falsely encouraged to believe that success is within
our grasp if we will work hard enough. "The fact is
that what is supposed to be and what is true of American history are two very different things."[17] Instead of
democracy (an ideal which has little to do with actual
conditions—Nature does not allow for it), we have a
situation little different from that of an old-time king-
dom. Money and land still rule, the average American
is kept in near poverty and lied to, and the gap between
the rich and the poor becomes ever more incredible.
But, given the eternal swing of Nature, the defects in
American democracy cannot go unremedied, nor the
drift toward ever greater money control go unchecked.
Something must happen.

Dreiser more and more came to think that communism or some form of socialism was what would

happen. There are many reasons—not all of them clear—why Dreiser arrived at this conclusion. His own conception of Nature is, of course, based on a dialectic not unlike that of Marxist thought. Dreiser's pulsating cosmos readily allows for Marx's dialectical materialism and the long history of class struggle. In addition, communism did not present itself as a closed system, and in the 1930s many liberals were convinced that it could more readily adjust to the calamities Dreiser's Nature was always forcing on helpless man. Soviet communism thus seemed to Dreiser to be based on a more accurate conception of reality than that of American democratic capitalism, with its apparently fatal susceptibility to illusory notions of morality or of a just and benign God. And in trying to account for Dreiser's leftward drift, one can neither overlook the Progressive elements in Dreiser's writing (*Sister Carrie*, it is remembered, came out of the same social climate that produced Upton Sinclair's *The Jungle*) nor the sympathy for the impoverished and powerless that runs all the way back to his childhood.

Dreiser obtained a firsthand look at communist society when upon the invitation of the Soviet Union's Bureau of Cultural Relations he toured the USSR during the last three months of 1927. Permitted considerable freedom of inquiry and movement, he was struck by the vitality of Russia and the promise its new society seemed to afford; but, as always he had his hesitations. He objected to the occasionally oppressive cloak-and-dagger atmosphere compounded of censorship and social regulation. Nevertheless, when he returned to New York, he told the reporters who greeted him that, taking into account the breadlines forming in the United States even in that pre-Depression year, he preferred the Russian system. Although hastily written, the book Dreiser published about his Russian experiences, *Dreiser Looks at Russia,* indicates that his remarks to the press were not intended for their shock value alone.[18]

The Russian trip was followed by a long automobile journey across the United States in 1930, numerous magazine articles on social and political matters, and a greater interest in political activism. Dreiser became involved in the agitation over the case of Tom Mooney, a labor organizer who was serving a life sentence in San Quentin for allegedly killing ten persons in the bombing of the 1916 Preparedness Parade in San Francisco. Anti-union forces had been determined to get Mooney, and he was convicted in a trial that most certainly involved bribed witnesses, false testimony, and clear evidence (a photograph) that Mooney was elsewhere when the bombing occurred. Despite the efforts of Dreiser and many others, Mooney was not freed until January 1939, after spending twenty-two years in prison for a crime he probably did not commit.

In addition to taking part in the effort to free Mooney, Dreiser signed petitions, wrote letters, and donated money to organizations such as the American Civil Liberties Union, and publications such as *New Masses.* In the spring of 1931 he accepted the chairmanship of the National Committee for the Defense of Political Prisoners, a position that led to one of the most notorious incidents in his life, when that same year he led a delegation of NCDPP volunteers into Harlan County, Kentucky, to investigate the harassment of the union organizers in the coal fields there. The investigating group encountered open hostility from local officials, and Dreiser warned the committee members to be circumspect in their behavior—a warning that was outrageously hypocritical since Dreiser had brought an attractive woman friend (her real name was never disclosed—Dreiser introduced her as "Marie Pergain") along from New York. On November 7, when Dreiser returned to his hotel he was being watched. At 11 P.M. his companion was observed entering his room. Toothpicks were leaned against the door, and they remained undisturbed through the night. As a consequence, Dreiser and Marie Pergain were indicted on charges of adultery by the county grand jury. The alleged adulterers had already left for home, but the story was picked up by newspapers across the country, and the miners' troubles were overshadowed by the scandal Dreiser had foolishly brought upon himself. Fortunately, the charges came to nothing.

Dreiser did not let the Kentucky embarrassment disturb his devotion to leftist politics. In 1932 he voted for William Z. Foster, the Communist Party candidate for president (although Dreiser was for Roosevelt in the next election). And, in 1934, he supported Upton Sinclair's campaign for governor on the End Poverty in California (EPIC) ticket.

Increasing age slowed his active participation considerably, but he retained, with characteristic hesitation and many doubts, his leftist stance even through such events as Stalin's purges and the Russo-German pact of 1939 that dismayed so many Soviet sympathizers. American communism drew much of its strength during the 1930s from the USSR's anti-fascist position, but when Hitler and Stalin agreed to a mutual nonaggression treaty, leftist disillusionment with Mother Russia was audible. Dreiser, however, said some amazing and contrary things. He argued that the pact would mean more security for the USSR, that it showed Hitler was basically humanitarian, and that it was a threat only to England, a nation for which he had little love or sympathy. The subsequent Nazi invasion of Russia literally made Dreiser sick. He soon recovered, however, holding to his pro-Soviet position, and repeatedly expressing concern about the Russian side of the war. Finally, in 1945, he formally joined the Communist Party.

Two of Dreiser's nonfiction books date from his 1930s political phase. The first, and most important of them, is *Tragic America* (1931), whose title echoed that of his most successful novel. Intended as Dreiser's outline for reform, *Tragic America* is one of his sloppiest books. It was put together out of clippings and "research" by Dreiser and his female assistants. Not unexpectedly, it received bad reviews nearly all around (even from fellow-traveling reviewers who, while pleased with Dreiser's attack on capitalism, were not impressed by the liberties he took with the party line). In a manner much less thoughtful and tempered than in *Hey, Rub-A-Dub-Dub!*, Dreiser flails away at big business, the legal system, schools, churches, and overzealous police tactics. Stuart Chase, writing in the *New York Herald Tribune*, claimed to have found eighteen factual errors in a single chapter.[20] Bad as it is, *Tragic America* gives us one more image of Dreiser the meliorist insisting that America need not be as tragic as it is, and holding to his central view that the belief in illusions is at the bottom of most of our economic and social problems. Though it is generally riddled with errors, portions of *Tragic America* lead the reader to wish that Dreiser had been able or willing to put the book together more carefully; it could have been an important document in American social history.

The same is not true of *America Is Worth Saving*,

which came out in 1941. It is a book designed to show
the futility of America's entrance into another European war on the side of Great Britain. Dreiser's suspicions of the British are adequately summarized in the
title of one of his chapters, "Does England Love Us
as We Love England?" Other chapters, notably "What
Is Democracy?" and "What Are the Defects of American Democracy?" serve only to reiterate ideas that had
appeared over twenty years before in *Hey, Rub-A-Dub-
Dub!* Dreiser had difficulty making publishing arrangements for *America Is Worth Saving* (the original title
had been *Is America Worth Saving?*), and the book
came out only a few months before the Germans made
the central argument in the book obsolete by invading
Russia. His pro-Soviet sympathies forced him to advocate American involvement in the war. Though written
in collaboration with Cedric Belfrage, a young British
novelist (Dreiser paid Belfrage $1,000 for his assist-
ance), *America Is Worth Saving* once again features
some of Dreiser's characteristic political attitudes and
phobias.

Dreiser's resistance to rigid systems often made his
endorsement of communist programs impossible, and
he was never considered an acceptable ideologist by
the communist hierarchy in the United States. It is
doubtful that Dreiser actually wanted a communist
state in America. When asked to speak on the radio
on behalf of Earl Browder's candidacy as Communist
Party nominee in the 1940 presidential election, Dreiser
did so. But, while endorsing Browder, he nonetheless
said, "I'm not a Communist and I don't agree with
the entire program of the Communist Party."[21] Such
a statement is typical of many Dreiser made in trying
to clarify his political position. Because of his belief in
the pendulum of Nature, what Dreiser saw in com-

munism was a leftward movement that at the time was not only necessary but inevitable. But he also believed that when Nature is ready the reverse tendency will begin, the pendulum will swing back, and we must avoid the kinds of illusions that result from dogmatic acceptance of a set of beliefs, be they philosophical or political.

There is little in Dreiser's thinking that can be called original, and he was certainly deceived in conceiving of himself as anything but a novelist. The time he spent on his nonfiction books—especially the years he spent in the 1930s working on *The Formula Called Man*—was not time well spent. And even the thirty-two–page preface he wrote for *The Living Thoughts of Thoreau* (1939) is a haphazard piece of writing that fails to reveal much about either Thoreau or himself—despite his unusual conception of Thoreau as an intuitive scientist. Throughout Dreiser's work there is something many critics have referred to as "clumsiness." But what this is, as his nonfiction writing certainly reveals, is a tendency toward laziness, a reluctance to revise, an impatience that pleases few readers. Though *Hey, Rub-A-Dub-Dub!* and *Tragic America* cast valuable light on Dreiser's work and time, they are for the extremely patient reader only—and this is unfortunate.

6

Dreiser

Again

Oh, what is this
That knows the road I came?
—*"The Road I Came"*

Theodore Dreiser is buried in Lot 1132 of the Whispering Pines section of Forest Lawn Cemetery in Hollywood next to the grave of Tom Mix. American lives—and deaths—seem to abound in anomalies of this sort (one cannot help but wonder whether Dreiser would have been amused by it). But there is some poignancy in this coincidence, for when they were alive, the two men represented opposite tendencies in American culture.

Tom Mix's reputation rests on reiterated Wild West movie melodramas that, as Norman Mailer points out in *Why Are We in Vietnam?*, have led to a perversion of reality. Dreiser's reputation, on the other hand, is to a certain extent determined by his insistence on overturning the folktales, the melodramatic plotlines that have provided so much nourishment for public errors of all sorts. Yet now they are side by side: Tom Mix, the purveyor of illusions; Theodore Dreiser, the smasher of illusions.

The odd thing about the problem of explaining Dreiser is that he spent his whole life and much of his writing time trying to do the job for us. His autobiographical books are there, in all their frankness, for us to read. And all of his novels, especially *The "Genius,"* contain fragments of himself. Yet Dreiser remains mysterious and many formulas have been devised to categorize him. These range from the various dual personality theories to Richard Lehan's valuable statement that "Dreiser was unable to reconcile his own romantic aspirations with his belief in a world of physical limits, and this led in his fiction to the displaced character—the man whose desire for self-fulfillment is in conflict with his environment."[1] But the point should perhaps be that Dreiser is not so much a displaced character as he is simply displaced by any

124

psychological or thematic scheme that is set up in an attempt to explain him.

In Dreiser we have a writer who cannot easily be understood in terms of his reading, his environment, or his education. He seems to have been born know- ing things he did not have to learn. He knew little of literary history, yet his first novel became a turning point, a touchstone in American literature. Somehow, with nothing that can be read as a sense of direction, he found himself at "the crossroads of the novel."[2] He set up a permanent roadblock for the older writers of the genteel tradition and went on to lead the fight for freedom of expression that made possible, to a certain extent, the achievement of the whole genera- tion of writers that followed him. As Mencken wrote of him in a letter sent to be read at Dreiser's funeral, "the fact remains that he was a great artist, and that no other American of his generation left so wide and handsome a mark upon the national letters. Ameri- can writing, before and after his time, differed as much as biology before and after Darwin."[3]

He was a man of contradiction and great incon- sistency in his own output. He could weld together a giant novel like *An American Tragedy* and follow it up by botching what could have been an important book, *Tragic America*. In his personal life he could sometimes be viciously cruel to his mistresses and his associates. At other times, as Sherwood Anderson indi- cates in an account of Dreiser visiting an orphanage and starting to cry as he saw the uniformed children come walking in,[4] the compassionate streak that is present in his fiction would overcome him. He could devote himself with great energy to contemporary de- velopments in politics and science, yet his verse col- lections—*Moods, Cadenced and Declaimed* (1928),

The Aspirant (1929), and *Epitaph* (1929) show little awareness of what was happening in poetry at that time.

But the difficulty in understanding Dreiser is as it should be. He was forever suspicious of systems, of easy ways of getting light into dark corners, of accepting theories. He viewed himself as, and indeed was, a product of the Nature that figures so prominently in his philosophy. The mystery and wonder and terror that Dreiser in *Hey, Rub-A-Dub-Dub!* associates with all life are apparent in any reading of Dreiser's own life. And the restless swinging from one extreme to another that defines Nature in Dreiser's thought could be used to explain the significance of his place in the development of the novel. He was what he was, when he was, where he was, because that is the way things are. That is as close as Dreiser could come to understanding himself, and it is perhaps as close as we can come. At his funeral, Charlie Chaplin read Dreiser's poem "The Road I Came."

> Oh, space!
> Change!
> Toward which we run
> So gladly,
> Or from which we retreat
> In terror—
> Yet that promises to bear us
> In itself
> Forever.
> Oh, what is this
> That knows the road I came?[5]

Notes

1. DREISER HIMSELF

1. Theodore Dreiser, *Dawn* (New York, 1931), p. 465.
2. Letter from H. L. Mencken (May 13, 1916).
3. Alfred Kazin, "Introduction," *The Stature of Theodore Dreiser*, eds. Alfred Kazin and Charles Shapiro (Bloomington, 1955), p. 5.
4. See Ellen Moers, *Two Dreisers* (New York, 1969).
5. See W. A. Swanberg, *Dreiser* (New York, 1965).
6. *Dawn*, p. 566.
7. Swanberg, p. 80.
8. Swanberg, p. 103.
9. Frank Harris, *Contemporary Portraits*, Second Series (New York, 1919), p. 91.
10. Swanberg, p. 376.
11. Letter from Dreiser to Charles G. Ross (August 16, 1909).
12. Swanberg, p. 118.
13. *Dawn*, p. 588.

2. DREISER'S WOMEN

1. Theodore Dreiser, *Sister Carrie* (Cleveland and New York, 1927), p. 1.

2. *Sister Carrie*, p. 2.
3. *Sister Carrie*, p. 84.
4. William A. Friedman, "A Look at Dreiser as an Artist: The Motif of Circularity in Sister Carrie," *Modern Fiction Studies* 8 (1963): 386.
5. *Sister Carrie*, p. 72.
6. *Sister Carrie*, p. 72.
7. F. O. Matthiessen, *Theodore Dreiser*, The American Men of Letters Series (New York, 1951), p. 73.
8. James T. Farrell, "Dreiser's 'Sister Carrie,'" *The Stature of Theodore Dreiser*, eds. Alfred Kazin and Charles Shapiro (Bloomington, 1955), p. 186.
9. *Sister Carrie*, p. 83.
10. *Sister Carrie*, p. 98.
11. *Sister Carrie*, p. 287.
12. *Sister Carrie*, p. 554.
13. Yoshinobu Hakutani, "*Sister Carrie* and the Problem of Literary Naturalism," *Twentieth Century Literature* 13 (1967): 7.
14. Philip Rahv, "Notes on the Decline of Naturalism," *Documents of Modern Literary Realism*, ed. George J. Becker (Princeton, 1963), p. 584.
15. Stuart P. Sherman, "The Barbaric Naturalism of Mr. Dreiser," *The Stature of Theodore Dreiser*, p. 80.
16. Donald Pizer, "Nineteenth-Century American Naturalism: An Essay in Definition," *Bucknell Review* 13 (December, 1965): 3.
17. Christopher G. Katope, "*Sister Carrie* and Spencer's *First Principles*," *American Literature* 41 (1969): 75.
18. Hakutani, p. 16.
19. Robert Penn Warren, *Homage to Theodore Dreiser* (New York, 1971), p. 19.
20. Yoshinobu Hakutani, "Dreiser and French Realism," *Texas Studies in Language and Literature* 6 (1964): 201.
21. Hakutani, p. 201.

22. Theodore Dreiser, *Dawn* (New York, 1931), p. 589.
23. Eliseo Vivas, "Dreiser, an Inconsistent Mechanist," *The Stature of Theodore Dreiser*, p. 241.
24. David Brion Davis, "Dreiser and Naturalism Revisited," *The Stature of Theodore Dreiser*, p. 226.
25. Davis, p. 230.
26. Charles Child Walcutt, "Theodore Dreiser and the Divided Stream," *The Stature of Theodore Dreiser*, p. 269.
27. *Sister Carrie*, p. 3.
28. Robert H. Elias, *Theodore Dreiser: Apostle of Nature* (New York, 1949), p. 109.
29. Louisville *Times* (November 30, 1900), *The Stature of Theodore Dreiser*, p. 54.
30. Jack Salzman, "The Publication of *Sister Carrie*: Fact and Fiction," *Library Chronicle* 33 (University of Pennsylvania, 1967): 124.
31. Salzman, p. 131.
32. Sheldon Norman Grebstein, "Dreiser's Victorian Vamp," *Midcontinent American Studies Journal* 4 (1963): 5.
33. Sinclair Lewis, "Nobel Prize Acceptance Speech," *The Man from Main Street*, eds. Harry E. Maule and Melville H. Cane (New York, 1953), p. 8.
34. Philip L. Gerber, *Theodore Dreiser*, Twayne's United States Authors Series (New York, 1964), p. 77.
35. Theodore Dreiser, *Jennie Gerhardt* (Cleveland and New York, 1926), pp. 420-21.
36. *Jennie Gerhardt*, p. 431.
37. Gerber, p. 85.
38. W. A. Swanberg, *Dreiser* (New York, 1965), p. 146.
39. Swanberg, p. 123, p. 129.
40. Warren, pp. 46-47.
41. Letter from Dreiser to H. L. Mencken (April 8, 1919).
42. Matthiessen, p. 85.

3. DREISER'S MEN

1. Theodore Dreiser, *The "Genius"* (Cleveland and New York, 1943), p. 37.
2. *The "Genius,"* p. 736.
3. *The "Genius,"* p. 127.
4. *The "Genius,"* p. 285.
5. *The "Genius,"* p. 682.
6. Claude Bowers, *My Life* (New York, 1962), p. 156.
7. See Philip L. Gerber, *Theodore Dreiser,* Twayne's United States Authors Series (New York, 1964), pp. 111-112; F. O. Matthiessen, *Theodore Dreiser,* The American Men of Letters Series (New York, 1951), p. 159; and Robert Penn Warren, *Homage to Theodore Dreiser* (New York, 1971), p. 52.
8. *The "Genius,"* p. 724.
9. *The "Genius,"* p. 558.
10. Warren, p. 151.
11. *The "Genius,"* p. 542.
12. W. A. Swanberg, *Dreiser* (New York, 1965), p. 193.
13. Matthiessen, p. 159.
14. Warren, p. 50.
15. John Berryman, "Dreiser's Imagination," *The Stature of Theodore Dreiser,* eds. Alfred Kazin and Charles Shapiro (Bloomington, 1955), p. 150.
16. Walter Blackstock, "The Fall and Rise of Eugene Witla: Dramatic Vision of Artistic Integrity in *The "Genius,'"* Language Quarterly 5 (1967): 15.
17. Matthiessen, pp. 164-65.
18. Warren, p. 56.
19. Theodore Dreiser, *The Financier* (Cleveland and New York, 1946), p. 5.
20. *The Financier,* p. 503.
21. Theodore Dreiser, *The Titan* (Cleveland and New York, 1925), p. 380.
22. *The Titan,* p. 551.
23. Swanberg, p. 173.

24. Theodore Dreiser, *The Stoic* (Cleveland and New York, 1947), p. 278.
25. Robert H. Elias, *Theodore Dreiser: Apostle of Nature* (New York, 1949), p. 304.
26. Matthiessen, p. 135.
27. Michael Millgate, "Theodore Dreiser and the American Financier," *Studi Americani* 7 (Rome, 1961): 140.
28. Warren, p. 76.
29. Swanberg, p. 162.
30. See Sidney Richman, "Theodore Dreiser's *The Bulwark*: A Final Resolution," *American Literature* 34 (1962): 235.
31. Theodore Dreiser, *The Bulwark* (New York, 1946), p. 300.
32. *The Bulwark*, p. 334
33. *The Bulwark*, pp. 316-17.
34. *The Bulwark*, p. 301.
35. Again, see Richman, p. 232.
36. Granville Hicks, "Theodore Dreiser and 'The Bulwark,'" *The Stature of Theodore Dreiser*, p. 223.
37. Theodore Dreiser, *The Hand of the Potter* (New York, 1918), p. 45.

4. DREISER'S EXPLANATION—
AN AMERICAN TRAGEDY

1. For an extensive discussion of these two novels, see Alexander C. Kern, "Dreiser and Fitzgerald as Social Critics," *Papers of the Midwest Modern Language Association*, ed. Sherman Paul (Iowa City, 1972), pp. 80-87.
2. Philip L. Gerber, *Theodore Dreiser*, Twayne's United States Authors Series (New York, 1964), p. 147.
3. Theodore Dreiser, *An American Tragedy* (New York, 1925), I, 5.

4. *An American Tragedy*, I, 14.

5. Robert Penn Warren, *Homage to Theodore Dreiser* (New York, 1971), p. 112.

6. *An American Tragedy*, II, 92.

7. *An American Tragedy*, II, 402.

8. *An American Tragedy*, II, 402.

9. Examples include Van Wyck Brooks's *America's Coming of Age* (1915), Harold Stearn's compendium entitled *Civilization in the United States* (1922), Waldo Frank's *Our America* (1919), and Vernon L. Parrington's *Main Currents in American Thought* (1927-30).

10. F. O. Matthiessen, *Theodore Dreiser*, The American Men of Letters Series (New York, 1951), p. 203.

11. Robert Shafer, " 'An American Tragedy': A Humanistic Demurrer," *The Stature of Theodore Dreiser*, eds. Alfred Kazin and Charles Shapiro (Bloomington, 1955), p. 124.

12. Warren, p. 138.

13. For a study of the relationship between Dreiser and Thoreau in terms of *An American Tragedy*, see Charles L. Campbell, *"An American Tragedy*: Or, Death in the Woods," *Modern Fiction Studies* 15 (1969): 251-59.

14. For an extensive study of the Aladdin motif, see the chapter "Arabian Nights" in Ellen Moers, *Two Dreisers* (New York, 1969), pp. 271-85.

15. For a limited study of this aspect of Dreiser's symbolism, see Lauriat Lane, Jr., "The Double in *An American Tragedy*," *Modern Fiction Studies* 12 (1966): 213-20.

16. Strother B. Purdy, *"An American Tragedy* and *L'Etranger*," *Comparative Literature* 19 (1967): 268.

17. This incident is fully described by Moers, p. 217.

18. John T. Flanagan, "Dreiser's Style in *An American Tragedy*," *Texas Studies in Language and Literature* 7 (1965): 286.

19. Warren, p. 118.
20. John J. McAleer, *Theodore Dreiser: An Introduction and An Interpretation* (New York, 1968), pp. 2-3.

5. DREISER'S PHILOSOPHY AND POLITICS

1. Letter from H. L. Mencken to Burton Rascoe (Summer, 1920).
2. Theodore Dreiser, *Hey, Rub-A-Dub-Dub!* (New York, 1920), p. 6.
3. *Hey, Rub-A-Dub-Dub!*, pp. 7-8.
4. *Hey, Rub-A-Dub-Dub!*, p. 10.
5. *Hey, Rub-A-Dub-Dub!*, p. 10.
6. *Hey, Rub-A-Dub-Dub!*, p. 2.
7. *Hey, Rub-A-Dub-Dub!*, p. 18.
8. *Hey, Rub-A-Dub-Dub!*, p. 22.
9. *Hey, Rub-A-Dub-Dub!*, p. 111.
10. *Hey, Rub-A-Dub-Dub!*, p. 136.
11. *Hey, Rub-A-Dub-Dub!*, p. 162.
12. *Hey, Rub-A-Dub-Dub!*, p. 178.
13. *Hey, Rub-A-Dub-Dub!*, p. 181.
14. *Hey, Rub-A-Dub-Dub!*, pp. 210-211.
15. *Hey, Rub-A-Dub-Dub!*, p. 211.
16. *Hey, Rub-A-Dub-Dub!*, p. 25.
17. *Hey, Rub-A-Dub-Dub!*, p. 27.
18. For a third-person account of Dreiser's travels in Russia, see Ruth Epperson Kennell, *Theodore Dreiser and the Soviet Union* (New York, 1969).
19. His earlier application, in 1933, was rejected by Earl Browder on ideological grounds.
20. Stuart Chase, New York *Herald Tribune Books* (January 24, 1932), cited by W. A. Swanberg, *Dreiser* (New York, 1965), p. 392.
21. Swanberg, p. 472.

6. DREISER AGAIN

1. Richard Lehan, *Theodore Dreiser: His World and His Novels* (Carbondale, 1969), p. xii.
2. See Lehan's chapter with that title, pp. 240-58.
3. Carl Bode, *Mencken* (Carbondale, 1969), p. 328.
4. Sherwood Anderson, *The Portable Sherwood Anderson*, ed. Horace Gregory (New York, 1949), pp. 557-58.
5. Theodore Dreiser, *Moods, Philosophical and Emotional* (New York, 1935), pp. 240-41.

Bibliography

1. WORKS BY THEODORE DREISER

NOVELS

Sister Carrie. New York: Doubleday, Page, 1900.
Jennie Gerhardt. New York: Harper, 1911.
The Financier. New York: Harper, 1912. Revised edition,
    New York: Boni & Liveright, 1927.
The Titan. New York: John Lane Company, 1914.
The "Genius." New York: John Lane Company, 1915.
An American Tragedy. New York: Boni & Liveright, 1925.
The Bulwark. Garden City: Doubleday, 1946.
The Stoic. Garden City: Doubleday, 1947.

SHORT STORIES

Free, and Other Stories. New York: Boni & Liveright,
    1918.
Chains. New York: Boni & Liveright, 1927.
Fine Furniture. New York: Random House, 1930.
The Best Short Stories of Theodore Dreiser. Edited by
    Howard Fast. Cleveland: World, 1947.
The Best Short Stories of Theodore Dreiser. Edited by
    James T. Farrell. Cleveland and New York: World,
    1956.

DRAMA

Plays of the Natural and the Supernatural. New York:
    John Lane Company, 1916.
The Hand of the Potter. New York: Boni & Liveright,
    1918.

POETRY

Moods, Cadenced and Declaimed. New York: Boni & Liveright, 1928. Revised edition, New York: Simon and Schuster, 1935.
The Aspirant. New York: Random House, 1929.
Epitaph: a poem. New York: Heron Press, 1929.

AUTOBIOGRAPHY

A Traveler at Forty. New York: Century, 1913.
A Hoosier Holiday. New York: John Lane Company, 1916.
A Book About Myself. New York: Boni & Liveright, 1922 (eighth edition and beyond titled *Newspaper Days*).
Dawn. New York: Liveright, 1931.

NONFICTION

Twelve Men. New York: Boni & Liveright, 1919.
Hey, Rub-A-Dub-Dub! New York: Boni & Liveright, 1920.
The Color of a Great City. New York: Boni & Liveright, 1923.
Dreiser Looks at Russia. New York: Liveright, 1928.
A Gallery of Women. New York: Liveright, 1929.
My City. New York: Liveright, 1929.
"What I Believe," *Forum* (November, 1929), pp. 279-81.
Tragic America. New York: Liveright, 1931.
"Presenting Thoreau," *Introduction to The Living Thoughts of Thoreau*. New York: Longmans, Green & Company, 1939, pp. 1-32.
America Is Worth Saving. New York: Modern Age Books, 1941.

LETTERS

Letters to Louise. Edited by Louise Campbell. Philadelphia: University of Pennsylvania Press, 1959.
Letters of Theodore Dreiser. Edited by Robert H. Elias. Philadelphia: University of Pennsylvania Press, 1959.

2. WORKS ABOUT THEODORE DREISER

BIBLIOGRAPHY

Atkinson, Hugh C. *Checklist of Theodore Dreiser.* Columbus: Charles E. Merrill, 1969.

McDonald, Edward D. *A Bibliography of the Writings of Theodore Dreiser.* Philadelphia: The Centaur Book Shop, 1928.

Miller, Ralph N. *A Preliminary Checklist of Books and Articles on Theodore Dreiser.* Kalamazoo; Western Michigan College Library, 1947.

Orton, Vrest. *Dreiseriana: A Book About His Books.* New York: The Chocurua Bibliographies, 1929.

BIOGRAPHIES

Dreiser, Helen. *My Life with Dreiser.* Cleveland and New York: World, 1951.

Dudley, Dorothy. *Forgotten Frontiers: Dreiser and the Land of the Free.* New York: Harrison Smith and Robert Haas, 1932.

Elias, Robert H. *Theodore Dreiser: Apostle of Nature.* New York: Alfred A. Knopf, 1949.

Swanberg, W. A. *Dreiser.* New York: Charles Scribner's Sons, 1965.

Tjader, Marguerite. *Theodore Dreiser: A New Dimension.* Norwalk: Silvermine Publishers, 1965.

GENERAL INTRODUCTIONS

Gerber, Philip L. *Theodore Dreiser.* New York: Twayne, 1964.

Lehan, Richard. *Theodore Dreiser: His World and His Novels.* Carbondale: Southern Illinois University Press, 1969.

Matthiessen, F. O. *Theodore Dreiser.* New York: William Sloane, 1951.

McAleer, John J. *Theodore Dreiser: An Introduction and Interpretation.* New York: Holt, Rinehart, and Winston, 1968.

Moers, Ellen. *Two Dreisers*. New York: Viking, 1969.

Rascoe, Burton. *Theodore Dreiser*. New York: Robert McBride & Company, 1926.

Shapiro, Charles. *Theodore Dreiser: Our Bitter Patriot*. Carbondale: Southern Illinois University Press, 1962.

The Stature of Theodore Dreiser. Edited by Alfred Kazin and Charles Shapiro. Bloomington: Indiana University Press, 1955.

Warren, Robert Penn. *Homage to Theodore Dreiser*. New York: Random House, 1971.

INTERPRETATIONS OF DREISER'S MAIN WORKS

Sister Carrie

Friedman, William A. "A Look at Dreiser as an Artist: The Motif of Circularity in *Sister Carrie*." *Modern Fiction Studies* 8 (1963): 384-92.

Grebstein, Sheldon Norman. "Dreiser's Victorian Vamp." *Midcontinent American Studies Journal* 4 (1963): 3-12.

Hakutani, Yoshinobu. "*Sister Carrie* and the Problem of Literary Naturalism," *Twentieth Century Literature* 13 (1967): 3-17.

Katope, Christopher G. "*Sister Carrie* and Spencer's *First Principles*." *American Literature* 41 (1969): 64-75.

Moers, Ellen. "The Finesse of Dreiser," *American Scholar* 33 (Winter 1963): 109-14.

Salzman, Jack. "The Publications of *Sister Carrie*: Fact and Fiction." *Library Chronicle* 33 (University of Pennsylvania): 119-33.

Simpson, Claude. "*Sister Carrie* Reconsidered." *Southwest Review* 44 (Winter 1959): 44-53.

Jennie Gerhardt

Shapiro, Charles. "*Jennie Gerhardt*: The American Family and the American Dream." *Twelve Original Essays on Great American Novels*, pp. 177-95. Edited by Charles Shapiro. Detroit: Wayne State University Press, 1958.

The "Genius"

Blackstock, Walter. "The Fall and Rise of Eugene Witla: Dramatic Vision of Artistic Integrity in *The 'Genius.'* " *Language Quarterly* 5 (1967): 15-18.

Kwiat, Joseph J. "Dreiser's *The 'Genius'* and Everett Shinn, The Ashcan Painter." PMLA (March 1952: 15-31).

A Trilogy of Desire

Millgate, Michael. "Theodore Dreiser and the American Financier." *Studi Americani* (Rome) 7 (1961): 133-45.

Wilson, William Edward. "The Titan and the Gentleman." *Antioch Review* 23 (1963): 25-34.

An American Tragedy

Campbell, Charles L. "An American Tragedy: Or Death in the Woods." *Modern Fiction Studies* 15 (1969): 251-59.

Flanagan, John T. "Dreiser's Style in *An American Tragedy.*" *Texas Studies in Language and Literature* 7 (1965): 285-94.

Howe, Irving. "Dreiser and Tragedy." *New Republic* 151 (25 July 1964): 25-28.

Lane, Lauriat, Jr. "The Double in *An American Tragedy.*" *Modern Fiction Studies* 12 (1966): 213-20.

Lehan, Richard. "*An American Tragedy:* A Critical Study." *College English* 25 (December 1963): 187-93.

Purdy, Strother B. "*An American Tragedy* and *L'Etranger.*" *Comparative Literature* 19 (1967): 252-68.

Samuels, Charles Thomas. "Mr. Trilling, Mr. Warren, and *An American Tragedy.*" *Yale Review* 53 (1964): 629-40.

The Bulwark

Richman, Sidney. "Theodore Dreiser's *The Bulwark:* A
Final Resolution." *American Literature* 34 (1962):
229-45.

OTHER BIOGRAPHICAL WORKS OF SPECIAL INTEREST

Haley, Carmen O'Neill. "The Dreisers." *Commonweal*
(7 July 1933): 265-67.
Huth, J. F., Jr. "Theodore Dreiser: 'The Prophet.'"
American Literature (May 1937): 208-17.
Kennell, Ruth Epperson. *Theodore Dreiser and the So-
viet Union.* New York: International Publishers,
1969.
Van Gelder, Robert. "Interview with Theodore Dreiser."
New York *Times* (16 March 1941): 2,16.

CRITICAL WORKS OF SPECIAL INTEREST

Blackstock, Walter. "Dreiser's Dramatization of Art, the
Artist, and the Beautiful in American Life." *South-
ern Quarterly* 1 (1962): 63-86.
Flanagan, John T. "Theodore Dreiser in Retrospect."
Southwest Review (Autumn 1946): 408-11.
Hakutani, Yoshinobu. "Dreiser and French Realism."
Texas Studies in Language and Literature 6 (1964):
200-12.
Hoffman, Frederick J. *The Twenties.* New York: Viking,
1955.
Markels, Julian. "Dreiser and the Plotting of Inarticulate
Experience." *Massachusetts Review* 11 (1961): 431-
48.
Phillips, William L. "The Imagery of Dreiser's Novels."
PMLA 78 (1963): 572-85.
Pizer, Donald. "The Problem of Philosophy in the Novel."
Bucknell Review (1970): 53-62.
Ross, Woodburn O. "Concerning Dreiser's Mind." *Amer-
ican Literature* (November 1946): 233-43.

Thomas, J. D. "Epimetheus Bound: Theodore Dreiser and the Novel of Thought." *Southern Humanities Review* 3 (1969): 346-57.

Wagner, Vern. "The Maligned Style of Theodore Dreiser." *Western Humanities Review* 19 (1965): 175-84.

Willen, Gerald. "Dreiser's Moral Seriousness." *University of Kansas City* Review (March 1957): 181-87.

Wycherley, H. Alan. "Mechanism and Vitalism in Dreiser's Nonfiction." *Texas Studies in Language and Literature* 11 (1969): 1039-49.

Index

142

Cowperwood trilogy, 17
Crane, Stephen, 9, 40
Critical reception of books,
      42–44, 48, 50, 61–
      62, 66, 69, 71, 80,
      89, 119
Criticism and Fiction
      (Howells), 18
"Culhane, the Solid Man,"
      80
*Custom of the Country,
      The* (Wharton),
      66–67

Darwin, Charles, influence
      of, 15, 39, 113, 125
*Daughter of the Philistines,
      A* (Boyesen), 66–67
Dawn, 9–10
Dee, Frances, 23
Delineator (magazine), 7,
      25–26
Dell, Floyd, 17, 23, 59
Detail, use of, 59, 67, 83
Dialogue, use of, 59, 60,
      64, 86, 102–3
Dickens, Charles, 28
"Doer of the Word, A,"
      80
Dos Passos, John, 14
Dostoevsky, Feodor, 106
"Double," use of, 101
Doubleday, and *The
      Bulwark,* 79–80
Doubleday, Frank, 18, 19
Doubleday, Mrs., 18–19
Doubleday, Page, and

Sister Carrie, 8,
      18–19, 25, 42
Dreiser, Helen Richardson
      (second wife),
      12–13, 20
Dreiser, John (father),
      3–4, 10, 14, 15, 45
Dreiser, Paul (brother).
      See Dresser, Paul
Dreiser, Sallie White (first
      wife), 12–13,
      101–2
Dreiser, Sarah (mother),
      3, 4, 10, 45, 49
Dreiser, Theodore
   childhood of, 3–4, 10
   education of, 5, 6
   marriages of, 12–13
   and nervous breakdown,
      13–14, 45
   personality of, 9–10,
      11–12, 14, 26, 28
   physical appearance of,
      11
   relationship of, with
      women, 11–12, 26,
      28, 49–50, 58, 61,
      125
Dreiser Looks at Russia,
      14, 116–17
Dresser, Paul, 10–11, 13–
      14, 62, 80

Eastman, Max, 17
Eisenstein, Sergei, 22
Elder, Donald B., 79–80
Elias, Robert H., 71